Confess your faults one to another, and pray one for another, that ye may be healed. **The effectual fervent prayer of a righteous man availeth much.**

James 5:16

THIS IS NOT A BOOK TO SIMPLY READ – IT IS A PRAYER BOOK.

IT IS FOR YOU TO PRAY THE WORDS THAT THIS BOOK CONTAINS

TAKE A POSTURE THAT YOU WOULD NORMALLY USE TO PRAY AND CREATE AN ATMOSPHERE OF PRAYER BEFORE BEGINNING.

PRAYERS THAT AVAILETH MUCH
THE PRAYER BOOK

PRAYERS THAT AVAILETH MUCH
The Prayer Book

By Apostle. Emmanuel A Adjei

Copyright ©2023 by E. A. Adjei

All rights reserved.

Unless otherwise stated, all scripture quotations are taken from the King James version.

Write to:

Apostle Emmanuel A Adjei

fofo275@hotmail.com

ISBN: 9798866163779

CONTENTS

	PAGE
INTRODUCTION	8
NOTE	12

FOUNDATIONAL
PRAYER OF **THANKSGIVING**	13
PRAYER FOR **THE FORGIVNESS OF SIN**	15
PRAYER FOR **GOD'S COVERING**	17

GENERAL
PRAYER TO **MARRY (MALE)**	18
PRAYER TO **MARRY (FEMALE)**	22
PRAYER REGARDING **TROUBLED MARRIAGES**	26
PRAYER AGAINST **DIVORCE/SEPARATION.**	30
GENERAL PRAYER ABOUT **ONE'S MARRIAGE**	35
PRAYER AGAINST **SOUL TIES**	37
PRAYER AGAINST **SPIRITUAL MARRIAGE (FEMALE)**	40
PRAYER AGAINST **SPIRITUAL MARRIAGE (MALE)**	43
PRAYER FOR **YOUR FAMILY**	46
PRAYER REGARDING **RUN AWAY CHILDREN**	50
PRAYER FOR **A JOB**	54
PRAYER FOR A **RESPONSE FROM A JOB APPLICATION OR INTERVIEW**	56
PRAYER FOR **GOD TO LEAD YOUR WAYS.**	58
PRAYER FOR **THE CURRENT OR THE NEXT YEAR**	60
PRAYER FOR **HEALING**	63
PRAYER AGAINST **DEMONIC ATTACKS.**	65

PRAYER AGAINST **WITCHES / WIZARDS AND WITCHCRAFT ACTIVITIES**	70
PRAYER AGAINST **ALTARS**	74
PRAYER TO **CAST OUT DEMONS FROM SELF**	77
PRAYER TO **CAST OUT DEMONS FROM A PERSON**	80
PRAYER TO **CAST OUT DEMONS FROM A PLACE**	83
PRAYER TO **SANCTIFY AND BLESS A PLACE / THING**	86
PRAYER FOR **GOD'S INTERVENTION IN A SITUATION**	87
PRAYER FOR **THE HOLY SPIRIT**	89
PRAYER TO **BE FILLED WITH THE HOLY SPIRIT**	90
PRAYER FOR **SALVATION**	91
PRAYER FOR **WISDOM, KNOWLEDGE & UNDERSTANDING**	92
PRAYER ABOUT **ONE'S MINDSET**	94
PRAYER FOR BEING **SUCCESSFUL AND PROSPEROUS**	96
PRAYER FOR **GOD'S BLESSING**	98
PRAYER TO **OBEY THE WORD OF GOD**	100
PRAYER FOR **THE MANIFESTATION OF GOD'S WORD**	102
PRAYER ABOUT **FINANCES**	105
PRAYER FOR **IMMIGRATIONAL DOOR**	107
PRAYER ABOUT **AN IMMIGRATION APPLICATION**	109
PRAYER WHEN **MINISTERING AT A CHURCH SERVICE**	111
PRAYER WHEN **WORKING AT A CHURCH SERVICE**	127
PRAYER WHEN **ATTENDING CHURCH SERVICE**	131

PRAYER FOR **CHURCH GROWTH**	134
GENERAL PRAYER **FOR A CHURCH**	139
PRAYER FOR **EVANGELISM**	144
PRAYER FOR A MAN OF GOD/PASTOR	149

INTRODUCTION

I believe that it is not a coincidence that you have an interest in this PRAYER BOOK. I believe that it is the doing of the Lord.
By the guidance and leading of the Holy Spirit, this prayer book has been written to help, lead and join people in prayer.

There is an eternal law which is that until one asks God in person or on behalf of someone, he or she will not receive from God.

Ask, and it shall be given you; seek, and ye shall find; knock, and it shall be opened unto you: For every one that asketh receiveth; and he that seeketh findeth; and to him that knocketh it shall be opened.

Matthew 7:7-8

For the one who does not know how to pray, this is one of God's ways of helping you to pray and making it possible for you to pray.

To the one who knows how to pray but is not fervent in prayer, this is one of God's ways of helping you to pray fervently and making it possible for you to pray.

To the one who knows how to pray fervently, this is one of God's ways of joining with you in prayer and making it possible for you to pray.

Not only for the above, but this prayer books will also stir up your spirit for fervent prayers and by it, God will release a grace on you to pray.

You will catch the prayer fire.
In Jesus Christ name.
The bible teaches us to pray about everything.

Be careful for nothing; but in everything by prayer and supplication with thanksgiving let your requests be made known unto God.
Philippians 4:6

It teaches that we should pray without ceasing.

Pray without ceasing.
1 Thessalonians 5:17

Our Lord and Saviour Jesus Christ was a master of persistent, fervent prayers. He persisted in prayer.

And he left them, and went away again, and prayed the third time, saying the same words.
Matthew 26:44

It teaches us also that it is the fervent prayer of a person that avails much.

Confess your faults one to another, and pray one for another, that ye may be healed. *The effectual fervent prayer of a righteous man availeth much.*

James 5:16

Prayer is what makes a difference. Prayer is the invisible power that is available to mankind, by which one can influence decisions and situations. In Peter and John's cases, you will notice that what made the difference between Peter and John's lives was prayer. John was killed but Peter was saved. The bible made us understand clearly that what made the difference was the fervent, persistent prayer of the church.

And he killed James the brother of John with the sword. And because he saw it pleased the Jews, he proceeded further to take Peter also. (Then were the days of unleavened bread.) And when he had apprehended him, he put him in prison, and delivered him to four quaternions of soldiers to keep him; intending after Easter to bring him forth to the people. Peter therefore was kept in prison: but prayer was made without ceasing of the church unto God for him. And when Herod

would have brought him forth, the same night Peter was sleeping between two soldiers, bound with two chains: and the keepers before the door kept the prison. And, behold, the angel of the Lord came upon him, and a light shined in the prison: and he smote Peter on the side, and raised him up, saying, Arise up quickly. And his chains fell off from his hands.

Acts 12:2-7

Until prayer goes up, nothing can come down.

As you use this PRAYER BOOK to pray, your prayers will ascend to heaven and God will hear them and answer in your favour.

By your prayers you will have an advantage and you will prosper.

NOTE:

- *This is not a book to simply read – it is a prayer book*
- *pray the words that the book contains*
- *take a posture that you would normally use to pray and pray*
- *Prayers in foundational list must be prayed first when you start praying.*
- *You can continue to use your own words to pray when you have finished praying on a particular subject.*
- *You can pray the same prayer points several times until you are released in the spirit, or you receive the answer.*
- *You can use the prayers in this book to pray for others by substituting their names.*
- *Allow the Holy Spirit to lead you on how to use this prayer book.*

PRAYER OF THANKSGIVING

Thank you Lord God Almighty.
Thank you, Precious Jesus.
Thank you, Holy Spirit.
God of Abraham, God of Isaac and God of Jacob, thank you for all that you have done and all that you're doing.
I thank you for your mercy, for your grace, for your loving kindness, your goodness and your favour.
Thank you for your provision, for your protection and your victory.
Thank you for last month and this month.
Thank you for all the plans you have for me, plans to prosper me and to give me a future, and a hope and not to harm me.
Father, I thank you for the name, Jesus and for your Holy Spirit.
I thank you for the power of the Holy Spirit.
I thank you for your salvation and for the forgiveness of sin.
I thank you for the answered prayers and testimonies.
Lord, thank you that, despite the challenges and the difficulties,
It would have been worse had you not been on my side.
Thank you, precious Jesus.

Thank you, sweet Holy Spirit.
Thank you, Jehovah.
Thank you, angels of the Lord.
Lord, may your name be glorified and may your name be exalted.
I praise your name.
In Jesus Christ name.
Amen

PRAYER FOR THE FORGIVNESS OF SIN

Father in heaven I ask for the forgiveness of sin.
God Almighty I repent of my sins, and I ask that you forgive me of my sins and trespasses.
Any sin that I've committed against you, myself, or any being, knowing or unknowing, willing or unwilling, I repent of it and I ask that forgive me of those sins.
Wash me with the blood of Jesus, cleanse me and acquit me of these sins.
Father, I ask in the name of Jesus, that you deliver me form all evil effects and consequences of my sins.
I also ask that you deliver all whom I have sinned against, from the evil effects and consequences of my sins.
Father, I ask that you continue to show me and convict me of my sins
By your Spirit and your power
Deliver me from those sins and set me free from those sins.
Let me know sin for what it is and how destructive it is.
Deliver me from temptations, challenges, weaknesses, difficulties, circumstances, and ignorance that lead me into sin.

Father, let my sins of today be no more.
Father, I thank you for this forgiveness of sin.
In Jesus Christ name I have prayed.
Amen

PRAYER FOR GOD'S COVERING/PROTECTION

My Father in heaven, in the name of Jesus by the power of the Holy Ghost,
I soak my body, my spirit, my soul and my life in the blood of Jesus and I surrounded myself with the Holy Ghost consuming fire.
I wear the full amour of God as it is in Ephesians 6.
Lord God Almighty I ask that wear me your complete amour.
Cover me as the hen covers its chicks and form a hedge around me.
Father in heaven I also bring before you all that is connected to me
And all that I am involved in, including my family
And I soak them in the blood of Jesus, and I surround them with the Holy Ghost consuming fire.
Lord God Almighty cover them as the hen covers its chicks
And form a hedge around them and wear them your complete amour.
In Jesus Christ name I have prayed
Amen

PRAYER TO MARRY (MALE)

Father in heaven in the name of Jesus I pray to you.
Father in heaven I thank you for today and for my life.
I thank you for creating marriage.
Father, I desire to marry, therefore I ask that you give me a wife.
I ask that you help me to marry.
I ask that lead me to find that woman whom I will love and who will also love me.
Order my steps and direct me to that one woman,
That one person that is for me and together we will remain married until you call us into eternity.
Wherever this woman is I ask that let us cross paths and let us recognise one another.
Father, forgive me of any sexual sins that I have committed.
Also forgive me of all unfaithfulness in my previous relationships.
I repent of it.
Father, I ask that deliver me from any marital covenant that I am in that has been preventing me from marriage.
I also ask that you deliver me from any spiritual marriage that I am in, knowing or unknowing.
Father your Word says that in the last days many will be forbidden to marry.

I ask that deliver me from whatever or whoever has forbidden me to marry.
Save me from these things.
Satan, I command you in the name of Jesus to take your hands off my marriage.
I bind you and rebuke you regarding it, in the name of Jesus.
You demons that have hijacked my marriage and are forbidding me from marrying,
I bind you now and command you to take your hands off my marriage now, in Jesus Christ name.
You evil spirit that have married me and is preventing me from marrying, I reject you in the name of Jesus.
Whatever covenants, oaths, tokens or activities which gave you right against my marriage,
I denounce them now in Jesus Christ name.
I cancel them now in the name of Jesus, by the blood of Jesus.
Any altars, high places, strongholds, walls of Jericho or gates of bronze against my marriage, scatter by fire now.
Let there be a violent earthquake to crumble you, in Jesus Christ name.
Father in heaven deliver and save me from them.
Angels of the Lord go and bring my marriage; I accept and take it now in Jesus' name.
Father, I ask that deliver me from any mindsets, thought patterns, imaginations, knowledge,

understanding, misunderstanding and lies that have prevented me from marriage.

Father, I also ask that you deliver me from any attitude, character, temperament and personality that is preventing me from marrying.

Grant unto me whatever knowledge, wisdom and understanding that I need to marry.

Show unto me whatever I need to start or stop in order for me to marry.

Let me find favour before you and find favour before the woman who is for me to marry.

Your Word says it is not good for man to be alone. It is not good for me to be alone, therefore help me to find a wife.

Your Word says that because of sexual immorality each one of us should marry.

I ask that you help me to marry so that I will be free from the sin of sexual immorality.

Give unto me that woman who is the flesh of my flesh and bone of my bones.

As you helped Isaac to find a wife, help me to find a wife.

Oh, you my wife to be, whoever you are and wherever you are,

It is the will of God for me to marry,

For the scripture says that marriage is honourable,

Therefore, I command you to come out of the shadows for me to meet you, in the name of Jesus.

In the name of Jesus, I loose you from anything that has bound you

And forbidden you to marry now, by fire.
I command the Holy Ghost fire to consume
anything that has covered you, in the name of Jesus.
Satan, I bind you regarding her now, in Jesus Christ name.
Father, set her free and bring her.
Father, when we cross paths may we recognise each other and may we accept each other as a couple.
May our souls be knitted together and may our relationship lead to marriage.
Father, save me from being deceived or blinded,
So that I do not marry the wrong person.
In Jesus Christ name I have prayed.
Amen

PRAYER TO MARRY (FEMALE)

Father in heaven in the name of Jesus I pray to you.
Father in heaven I thank you for today and for my life.
I thank you for creating marriage.
Father, I desire to marry therefore I ask that you give me a husband.
I ask that you help me to marry.
I ask that you let me be found by the man whom I will love and who will also love me.
Order my steps and direct me to that one man.
Position me to be located and chosen by that one man that is for me and together we will remain married until you call us into eternity.
Wherever this man is I ask that you let us cross paths and recognise one another.
Father, forgive me of any sexual sins that I have committed.
Forgive me also of all unfaithfulness in my previous relationships.
I repent of it.
Father, I ask that you deliver me from any marital covenant that I am in that has prevented me from marrying.
I also ask that you deliver me from any spiritual marriage that I am in, knowing or unknowing.

Father your Word says that in the last days many will be forbidden to marry.

I ask that you deliver me from whatever or whoever has forbidden me to marry.

Save me from these things.

Satan, I command you in the name of Jesus to take your hands off my marriage.

I bind and rebuke you regarding it, in the name of Jesus.

You demons that have hijacked my marriage and have forbidden me to marry, I bind you now and I command you to take your hands off my marriage, in Jesus Christ name.

You evil spirit that has married me and prevented me from marrying, today I reject you in the name of Jesus.

Whatever covenants, oaths, tokens or activities which gave you an open door against my marriage, I denounce you now in the name of Jesus.

I cancel them now in the name of Jesus, by the blood of Jesus.

Any altars, high places, strongholds, walls of Jericho or gates of bronze against my marriage, scatter by fire now.

Let there be a violent earthquake to crumble you, in Jesus Christ name.

Father in heaven, deliver and save me from them.

Angels of the Lord go and bring my marriage, I accept and take it now, in Jesus' name.

Father, I ask that deliver me from any mindsets, thought patterns, imaginations, knowledge, understanding, misunderstanding and lies
That have prevented me from marriage.
Father I also ask that you deliver me from any attitude, character, temperament and personality
That is preventing me from marring.
Grant unto me the knowledge, wisdom and understanding that I need to marry.
Show unto me whatever I need to start or stop in order to marry.
Let me find favour before you and find favour before the man who is for me to marry.
Your Word says that it is not good for man to be alone, therefore you made him a helper.
It is not good for me to be alone and not be the helper that you made me to be, therefore let me be found by the husband I am to marry.
Your Word says that because of sexual immorality each one of us should marry.
I ask that you help me to marry so that I will be free from the sin of sexual immorality.
Give unto me that man whom I am to be the flesh of his flesh and bone of his bone.
As you caused Rebekah to be found for Isaac, so I ask that let me be found and chosen by that man.
Oh, you my husband to be, whoever you are and wherever you are,
It is the will of God for me to marry,
For the scripture says that marriage is honourable.

I therefore command you to come out of the shadows for me to meet you, in the name of Jesus.
In the name of Jesus, I loose you from anything that has bound you
And forbidden you to marry now, by fire.
I command the Holy Ghost fire to consume anything that has covered you in the name of Jesus.
Satan, I bind you regarding him now, in Jesus Christ name.
Father set him free and bring him.
Father when we cross paths may we recognise and accept each other as a couple.
May our souls be knitted together and may our relationship lead to marriage.
Father, save me from being deceived or blinded, that I may not marry the wrong person.
In Jesus Christ name I have prayed.
Amen

PRAYER REGARDING TROUBLED MARRIAGES

Almighty God, I bring the troubles of my marriage before you right now in the name of Jesus and I ask for your divine intervention.

Whatever and whoever the cause of these troubles are,

I rebuke and command them to wither right now in the name of Jesus Christ, by the power of the Holy Spirit.

I reject these troubles from my marriage, in the name of Jesus.

Father in heaven I ask that may you deliver this marriage

From whatever causes or reasons behind the troubles right now.

Whatever storm is behind the troubles of this marriage

I rebuke it and command it to wither now, in the name of Jesus.

I command the storm to cease against this marriage right now.

Whatever powers, human beings, spirit beings or schemes are behind the troubles of this marriage,

I rebuke all, in the name of Jesus Christ of Nazareth and by the power of the Holy Ghost,

I command you to loose your grip and go to the abyss right now, in the name of Jesus.
Lord God Almighty, you know why this trouble
You understand this trouble.
Father, may you intervene right now
And deliver this marriage from whatever is troubling it.
Lord, I pray that may me and my spouse be of one body, one soul, one mind and one speech.
May we not be divided, but may we be united.
May we understand each other and not fight against each other.
Father, whatever confusion or behaviours that have transpired and by that this marriage is in turbulence, I ask that you intervene and deliver this marriage from its troubles.
Father help and cause us to forgive one another.
Help and cause us to understand one another.
Help us and cause us to make peace with one another.
Whatever I need to stop or start doing for this marriage to continue in joy, show it to me and help me do it.
Whatever my partner needs to stop or start doing for this marriage to continue in joy, show it to him/her and help him/her to do it.
Father step into this marriage.
Do not let this marriage lead to separation or divorce.

In the name of Jesus, any spirit that has been sent against this marriage, to cause this marriage to fail, I bind you right now and by the power of the Holy Ghost, I command you to loose your grip now and go to the abyss.

Whatever evil you have set in motion already against this marriage,
I halt it now and I reverse it back to sender, in the name of Jesus by the power of the Holy Ghost.

Let the Lord arise and may His enemies be scattered and they that hate him be destroyed.

Oh, your God arise and let the enemies of our marriage be scattered and they that hate our marriage be destroyed; let their end be now.

You spirit of confusion; I bind you in the name of Jesus by the power of the Holy Ghost regarding this marriage
And I rebuke and command you come out of my marriage and be gone now in the name of Jesus.

Lord, anything that has been done to scramble the words we speak to one another, to cause misunderstanding, misrepresentation and confusion
And to cause us to be perceived as rude, arrogant or harsh towards each other,
I reject and cancel it in the name of Jesus
And I forbid it to succeed in our marriage again.
Father, deliver us from it.

Almighty God, cause us to understand each other's words.
Cause us to understand each other.

Let us love one another.
Let us be patient with one another.
Help us to treat one another as we ourselves would want to be treated.
Help us tolerate one another.
Let us desire one another all the more.
God, I know you hate divorce for your word says so,
Therefore, I pray that you have mercy on us, intervene and stabilise this marriage.
May our marriage never lead to separation or divorce.
As the days, months, years and seasons go by, may you cause this marriage to remain and become more and more stable.
In Jesus Christ name I have prayed.
Amen

PRAYER AGAINST DIVORCE/SEPARATION

My father in heaven, I thank you for my marriage and for my partner.

Lord God Almighty I thank you because despite the difficulties, it would have been worse without you.

Father, I bring my marriage before you and I ask that you save my marriage from separation and divorce.

Whatever the reason why our marriage is leading to divorce and separation, I ask that you deliver us from it.

Deliver us from any hurts, offences and wounds and cause us to forgive one another and heal us from this.

Deliver us from any misunderstandings, delusions and lies that are leading us to separation and divorce.

Deliver us from any demonic attacks and systems that are leading us to separation and divorce.

Deliver us from any demons and human vessels that are leading us to separation.

Father your Word says how can two walk together, unless they agree.

Deliver us from any disagreements and cause us to agree.

May me and my partner be of one body, one spirit, one soul, one mind and one speech as a couple.

May we never be in disunity.
Lord God Almighty, deliver our marriage from whatever or whoever is causing this separation or divorce.
Anything that I need to know or to stop or start doing in order for this marriage not to end in separation or divorce,
I ask that you show it to me and help me to do it, in the name of Jesus.
Anything that my partner needs to know or to stop or start doing in order for this marriage not to end in separation or divorce,
I ask that you show it to him/her and help him/her to do it, in the name of Jesus.
Father, I ask that revive our love for one another.
Cause us to desire one another and not want to separate or divorce.
Satan, I bind you regarding my marriage.
I command you in the name of Jesus to take your hands off me, my partner and our marriage.
You demons behind the divorce and separation of my marriage,
I bind you now in the name of Jesus
And I command you to leave and go to the abyss now by fire, by the power of the Holy Ghost.
Whatever you have set in motion against our marriage,
I halt it now and reverse it back to sender, in Jesus Christ name.

You spirit of confusion, I bind you now in the name of Jesus, come out of me now.
Come out of my partner now.
Come out of my marriage now and go to the abyss in Jesus Christ name by fire, by fire, by fire.
Go with all that is of you.
I reverse every evil you have set in motion against our marriage now, in Jesus Christ name.
Any storm that is blowing against me and my partner and our marriage,
I rebuke the power behind it now, in the name of Jesus
And I command the storm to cease now by the power of the Holy Ghost.
Any enchantments, divinations, spells, curses, hexes, charms, magic, witchcraft activities, delusions and hypnotisms against our marriage,
I revoke it now in the name of Jesus.
By the blood of Jesus, I cancel and nullify all now.
Whatever evil these activities have set in motion against our marriage,
I halt and reverse back to sender.
Any altars, high places, poles, shrines, walls of Jericho, gates of bronze and strongholds
That have been established against our marriage,
I command them to scatter now, in the name of Jesus;
Crumble now by a violent earthquake, by the power of the Holy Ghost.

Whatever evil you have set in motion against our marriage I halt and reverse it back to sender.
Oh Lord, fight against those who are fighting against our marriage.
Contend against those who are contending against our marriage.
Let them be destroyed.
Take up your shield and javelin and come to our aid.
Save our marriage.
Do not allow our family to break down by separation or divorce.
I ask for your intervention in our marriage; that you save it from divorce.
Turn it into a happy marriage.
Whatever wrestling is going on against me, my partner and our marriage by powers, principalities, rulers of the darkness of this world and spiritual wickedness,
I ask that wrestle against them and deliver us from their grip.
Grant us victory over them.
Holy Spirit, I summon anyone who is behind this divorce and separation to you.
Father, I ask for your judgement against them.
Arise and judge them now.
I declare and decree, in the name of Jesus that our marriage will not break down, we will not separate or divorce.
But we will be more united and rather love each other more.

That we will understand each other more. in the name of Jesus by the power of the Holy Spirit.
Father be gracious unto us by saving our marriage.
Show me your loving kindness my saving our marriage.
Be merciful to my partner by saving our marriage.
Jesus as you released new wine in the marriage in Canaan when their wine was finished, I ask that you come and release new wine into my marriage.
Forever restock my marriage with your sweet wine, that our marriage will be sweet again.
I thank you for an answered prayer, in Jesus Christ name.
Amen

GENERAL PRAYER ABOUT ONE'S MARRIAGE

Father in heaven I thank you.
I thank you for my partner and for my marriage.
Father, into your hands I commit my marriage.
I ask in the name of Jesus that you protect my marriage.
Form a hedge of fire around it.
Father, deliver my marriage from any evil spirit or person that destroys marriages.
I also ask that deliver my marriage from demonic and evil schemes that destroy marriages.
Oh Lord, let the things that have destroyed people's marriages in this community, nation and the world be unable to destroy my marriage.
May it not succeed in my marriage.
Father, save my marriage from myself and from my partner.
Let us not destroy our own marriage.
I ask that cause me and my partner to love each other more.
Let us understand each other more.
As the days and seasons go by,
May you cause us to desire one another more.
May we be united and never divided.
Let us be of one body, one spirit, one soul and one speech.

Father, grant us the knowledge, wisdom and understanding needed to have a very successful marriage.

Holy Spirit, I summon anyone who is fighting against our marriage to you.

Father, I ask for your judgement against anyone who has risen or will arise against our marriage.

Arise and judge them.

But hide our marriage and cover it.

Make it flourish.

Let it be established forever.

Sustain our marriage by your grace and mercy.

I declare and decree in the name of Jesus, that our marriage will never end in divorce or separation.

We will never be at logger heads.

We will love and desire one another all the more, by the power of the Holy Spirit.

Father, grant us the attitude, character and mindset that it takes to remain married.

Deliver us from familiarity towards one another and let us not take each other for granted.

Jesus, as you released new wine in the marriage in Canaan when their wine finished,

I ask that you release new wine into my marriage.

Forever restock my marriage with your sweet wine.

Thank you for an answered prayer, in Jesus Christ name.

Amen

PRAYER AGAINST SOUL TIES

Lord have mercy on me and forgive me of my sins. Please acquit me of my sins by the blood of Jesus.
Lord, have mercy on me for the wrongs and errors from the past that have put me in this situation.
I command every soul tie to break from my life now by the fire of the Holy Spirit.
I pronounce divorce against any soul tie in the name of Jesus.
I command soul ties to break from my life by fire in the name of Jesus.
I pronounce divorce from any soul tie by grace in the name of Jesus.
I RENOUNCE, BREAK AND DESTROY EVERY AGREEMENT THAT HAS BROUGHT US TOGETHER, now by the blood of Jesus.
I repent of any sexual immorality that I have been involved in.
Father, deliver me from any sexual immorality from my past that has brought about this soul tie.
Father, deliver me from any sexual escapades that I have been involved in; that my body, spirit and soul have tasted, and even still desires, that have created this soul tie.
I reject these desires and command them to die in my body, spirit and soul, in the name of Jesus by the blood of Jesus.

Lord God Almighty, deliver me from the memories of them forever.

By the covenant blood of Jesus I cancel and terminate any covenant between me and anyone that I have a soul tie with.

By the covenant blood of Jesus I cancel and terminate any marriage covenant between me and anyone that I have a soul tie with.

This day I return by fire, every token and property of a soul tie that is in my custody – whether spiritually, physically, sexually, emotionally or mentally, in the name of Jesus.

Lord let your fire visit every fowl certificate, recording and guidance where my name has been written as a partner or soul tie and wipe it off now, in the name of Jesus.

Lord by your blood, I flush out every dispute from my spirit, soul and body, be it spiritually, physically or anywhere else now, in the name of Jesus.

Fire of God visit my life and my body and destroy that negative thing that is attracting and causing this soul tie now, in the name of Jesus.

From this day on, create a gap wall of protection between me and anyone that I have a soul tie with, by fire.

Spirit of God, help me not to go back to the things that opened the door for any soul tie and anything which has caused a soul tie to come back, in the name of Jesus I pray.

Father in heaven please restore unto me all that I lost because of this soul tie.
In Jesus Christ name I have prayed, I thank you for an answered prayer.
Amen

PRAYER AGAINST SPIRITUAL MARRIAGE (FEMALE)

Lord have mercy on me and forgive me of my sins. Please acquit me of my sins by the blood of Jesus. Lord, have mercy on me for the wrongs and errors from the past that have put me in this situation, that have caused this spirit to come and have sex with me.

I command this spirit that comes to have sex with me to break from my life, now by the fire of the Holy Spirit.

I pronounce divorce against this spirit in the name of Jesus.

I command any spiritual marriage to break from my life by fire, in the name of Jesus.

I pronounce divorce between my soul and this spirit, by grace in the name of Jesus.

I RENOUNCE, BREAK AND DESTROY EVERY AGREEMENT THAT HAS BROUGHT US TOGETHER now, by the blood of Jesus.

I repent of any sexual immorality that I have been involved in.

Father, deliver me from any sexual immorality from my past that has brought about this spiritual marriage.

Father, deliver me from any sexual escapades that I have been involved in; that my body, spirit and soul have tasted, and even still desires, that have created this soul tie.

I reject these desires and command them to die in my body, spirit and soul, in the name of Jesus by the blood of Jesus.

By the sword of the Spirit, I cut off the penis of this spirit that comes to have sex with me now in the name of Jesus, by the power of the Holy Ghost.

Lord God Almighty, close any door and cancel any right of entry for this spirit to come and have sex with me.

By the covenant blood of Jesus, I cancel and terminate any covenant between me and this spirit and anyone that I have a spiritual marriage with.

By the covenant blood of Jesus I cancel and terminate any marriage covenant between me and this spirit and anyone that I have a spiritual marriage with.

This day I return by fire, every token and property of a soul tie that is in my custody – whether spiritually, physically, sexually, emotionally or mentally, in the name of Jesus.

Lord let your fire visit every fowl certificate, recording and guidance where my name has been written as a partner or soul tie and wipe it off now, in the name of Jesus.

Lord Almighty, deliver me from any evil effects and consequences of any sexual immorality or sexual abuse that I have been involved in that has allowed this spirit.

Lord by your blood, I flush out every dispute from my spirit, soul and body,
Be it spiritually, physically or anywhere else now, in the name of Jesus.
Fire of God visit my life and my body and destroy that negative thing that is attracting and causing this spiritual marriage now,
In the name of Jesus.
From this day on, create a gap wall of protection between me and anyone that I have a spiritual marriage with, by fire.
Spirit of God, help me not to go back to the things that opened the door for this spirit
And anything which has caused a spiritual marriage to come back, in the name of Jesus I pray.
Father in heaven please restore unto me all that I lost because of these spirits.
Thank you for an answered prayer.
Amen

PRAYER AGAINST SPIRITUAL MARRIAGE (MALE)

Lord have mercy on me and forgive me of my sins. Please acquit me of my sins by the blood of Jesus. Lord, have mercy on me for the wrongs and errors from the past that have put me in this situation that have caused this spirit to come and have sex with me.

I command this spirit that comes to have sex with me to break from my life, now by the fire of the Holy Spirit.

I pronounce divorce against this spirit in the name of Jesus.

I command any spiritual marriage to break from my life by fire, in the name of Jesus.

I pronounce divorce between my soul and this spirit, by grace in the name of Jesus.

I RENOUNCE, BREAK AND DESTROY EVERY AGREEMENT THAT HAS BROUGHT US TOGETHER now, by the blood of Jesus.

I repent of any sexual immorality that I have been involved in.

Father, deliver me from any sexual immorality from my past that has brought about this spiritual marriage.

Father, deliver me from any sexual escapades that I have been involved in,

That my body, spirit and soul have tasted and even still desires, that have created and opened a door for this spirit.

I reject these desires and I command them to die in My body, spirit and soul in the name of Jesus, by the blood of Jesus.

Lord God Almighty, close any door and cancel any right of entry for this spirit to come and have sex with me.

By the covenant blood of Jesus I cancel and terminate any covenant between me and this spirit and anyone that I have a spiritual marriage with.

By the covenant blood of Jesus I cancel and terminate any marriage covenant between me and this spirit and anyone that I have a spiritual marriage with.

This day I return by fire, every token and property of a soul tie that is in my custody

Whether spiritually, physically, sexually, emotionally or mentally, in the name of Jesus.

Lord let your fire visit every fowl certificate, recording and guidance

Where my name has been written as a partner or soul tie and wipe it off now, in the name of Jesus.

Lord Almighty, deliver me from any evil effects and consequences of any sexual immorality or sexual abuse

That I have been involved in that has allowed this spirit.

Lord by your blood, I flush out every dispute from my spirit, soul and body,
Be it spiritually, physically or anywhere else now, in the name of Jesus.
Fire of God visit my life and my body and destroy that negative thing that is attracting and causing this spiritual marriage now, in the name of Jesus.
From this day on, create a gap wall of protection between me and anyone that I have a spiritual marriage with, by fire.
Spirit of God, help me not to go back to the things that opened the door for this spirit
And anything which has caused a spiritual marriage to come back, in the name of Jesus I pray.
Father in heaven please restore unto me all that I lost because of these spirits.
Thank you for answered prayer.
Amen

PRAYER FOR YOUR FAMILY

Father in heaven I thank you for your mercies and grace.
I thank you for my family.
Lord God almighty, despite the difficulties and challenges, if you had not been on our side, we would have been worse off.
Father in heaven, I bring my partner and children before you, including me and I commit ourselves into your hands as a family.
I pray that may you continue to be with this family and protect us.
As a family, may we never be divided nor scattered.
Let things that have scattered the families of this community, town, nation and world not succeed with us.
As a family I ask that may we be united and love one another.
May we be there for one another and support each other.
God, cause us to also love one another and have compassion towards one another.
Let your blessings be on this family.
Let us prosper as a family and as individuals.
Let us know you precious Jesus as a family and as individuals.
May we be a blessing to one another.

Deliver us from anything which is meant to bring the pain of disunity among us.
Make this family invisible to the forces of darkness.
Anything that is in my blood line and also in my partner's blood line that is evil;
Whether it be curses, pain, shame, failure or anything else which is undesirable and not of you,
I reject it and detach this family from it, in the name of Jesus by the blood of Jesus.
Father in heaven, deliver us from it and connect us to the blood line of Christ, through your covenant.
Father, lead us out of temptation and deliver us from evil.
May no evil be, before us.
I declare and decree, in the name of Jesus, that no weapon fashioned against this family shall prosper
And I refute every weapon of the enemy against this family.
Satan, I bind you regarding this family, in the name of Jesus.
I command you to take your hands off this family and I rebuke you regarding this family.
You demons that have been assigned against this family,
I bind you now and I command you to leave and go to the abyss now, in the name of Jesus.
Whatever your assignment is, I nullify it now in the name of Jesus.
Whatever evil that you have set in motion
I halt it now and reverse it

May it boomerang back to sender, in the name of Jesus.

Any storm blowing against my family, I command you to be still now and whatever power is behind it I bind you and command you to wither now by fire, in Jesus Christ name.

Any altars, high places or poles against this family, be destroyed now by fire and by a violent earthquake,

In Jesus Christ name.

Any evil words, predictions, desires, spells, curses or witchcraft activity against this family

I cancel it right now in the name of Jesus and I nullify it by the blood of Jesus.

Whatever you were enforcing or maintaining, I halt it and reverse it back to sender.

Any human who has been sent or is coming into our family to scatter it,

I block them now in the name of Jesus.

Father, prevent them from coming. Stop them.

If they should come, may they not succeed.

May they be found out.

Oh Lord God Almighty, deliver this family from all these beings, activities and systems.

Let them not succeed with this family.

Father, cover my family as the hen covers its chicks and form a hedge of fire around us.

Let this family grow from strength to strength.

From peace to peace.

From righteousness to righteousness.

I declare and decree that me and my family shall serve the Lord and we are for signs and wonders. In Jesus Christ name I have prayed. I thank you for and answered prayer.
Amen

PRAYER REGARDING RUN AWAY CHILDREN

Father in heaven, I thank you for your mercies and grace.
I give you glory and praise.
Father, I bring the issue of my child ………(Name) leaving home prematurely and cutting ties with me.
I ask that you Almighty God bring him/her back home and reunite us.
Wherever ………… (Name) is, I ask that work on him/her and convict them and turn their heart and mind towards returning home and uniting with me.
I ask that you deliver him/her from whatever transpired and caused ………… (Name) to leave home cutting ties with me.
Sweet Holy Spirit, give ………… (Name) a change of heart and mind that will cause him to return home and be united with me.
Satan, I bind you regarding my child ………… (Name) and I command you to take your hands off ………… (Name) right now, in the name of Jesus.
Take your hands off his/her returning back home and uniting with me now in the name of Jesus.
You demons behind my child ………… (Name) departure from home and cutting ties with me,

I bind you now in the name of Jesus, by the power of the Holy Spirit
And I command you to take your hands of ....(Name)
I command you to leave .... (Name) and go back to the abyss in Jesus Christ name, by fire.
Whatever you have done and set in motion to cause .... (Name) to depart from home and cut ties with me,
I cancel and nullify it right now, in the name of Jesus.
I halt it and reverse it back to sender.
Any spells, enchantments, curses, hypnotisms, manipulations, brainwashing, delusions, witchcraft activities…etc. that have caused this,
In the name of Jesus, by the blood of Jesus I cancel it now.
Whatever evil these activities have set in motion against my child .... (Name)
I halt them now and reverse them back to sender.
Any altars, high places, shrines, grooves, walls of Jericho or strongholds that have been established against my child .... (Name)
to bring this situation about,
I command it to be destroyed by fire,
by a violent earth quake, in the name of Jesus right now.
Whatever it has set in motion and is being maintained against me and my child ....(Name)
I halt it and reverse it back to sender now.

Angels of the Lord, go and bring my child back to our home now and reunite us.

Whatever I or any member of my house did wrong, to cause my child .... (Name) to leave,

I repent of it and I ask that forgive me, my Father in heaven.

Cause my child ....(Name) to forgive me and that person.

Heal my child and deliver him from all hurts and consequences of this wrong and cause my child to forgive.

In the name of Jesus, by the power of the Holy Spirit,

I call forth you my child ...., (Name) your body, spirit and soul, and I command you to return back home now and be united with me. (REPEAT 7 TIMES)

Whatever has bound you, I lose you from it now in the name of Jesus.

Father loose ....(Name) and return ....(Name) back home.

Turn ....(Name) heart towards me and turn my heart towards him/her.

Father, cause .... (Name) to come to his/her senses, as the prodigal son came to his senses.

And cause ....(Name) to return home, just as the prodigal son returned home.

And join .... (Name) with me, just as the prodigal son was joined to the father.

Oh Lord, have mercy on me and cause my child to return to me.
I declare and decree, in the name of Jesus, by the finger of God that
My child is returning home and uniting with me.
I welcome .... (Name) home now, in Jesus Christ name.
I thank you father in heaven for an answered prayer.
Amen

PRAYER FOR A JOB

Father in heaven I thank you and I give you glory.
I thank you for your mercies and grace.
Father, I ask that you help me to find a job as I seek for one.
Sweet Holy Spirit, I invite you to join me in seeking a job.
Father, lead and direct me to that one job that is for me.
The job that will be a blessing to me in every way.
The job that will allow me to serve you and also to contribute my portion to society.
The job that will make me live a fulfilled and financially abundant life.
Let me recognise the job and apply for it.
Father, when I apply for this job let my application or CV be favoured before all.
And let me be called for an interview.
When I am called for an interview let me be favoured before all and be given the job.
Anything on my application or CV that will cause it not to be chosen for interview, I cancel it now in the name of Jesus.
I nullify it by the blood of Jesus.
I blindfold the employer's eyes regarding it.
May they not recognise or consider it.

Father, I also ask that whatever I need to correct on my application or CV
In order for it to be chosen for an interview, show it to me and help me to correct it.
Any power, being, systems and activities saying no to this,
Let them be destroyed. May they not succeed.
Any wrestling that is going or will be going on against me getting a job,
I ask that wrestle and fight against them Lord.
Father in heaven, grant me victory over them.
In Jesus Christ name.
I thank you for the job and for the answered prayer.
Amen

PRAYER FOR A RESPONSE FROM A JOB APPLICATION OR INTERVIEW

Father in heaven I thank you for my life.
Lord God almighty, I thank you for the vacancy that I applied for.
I thank you for causing them to call me for an interview.
I bring the selection process of the company before you and I commit it into your hands.
I ask that let their selection process favour me.
Father, I ask that influence their systems, procedures and decisions in my favour.
Cause the employer to call and offer me the job.
Anything in connection to my interview which will cause them not to offer me the job, I nullify it in the name of Jesus.
Father, let it be considered as foolishness to reject me and may they call me.
Among all the short-listed applicants and all the people that were interviewed, may I be favoured.
Satan, I bind you regarding me from being offered the job.
Take your hands off it now, in the name of Jesus.
I revoke and cancel every evil and demonic influence that has been cast against me from being offered the job.

I declare and decree in the name of Jesus that I shall hear from them.

The outcome of the interview will be only one – that I will be offered the job.

In the name of Jesus, by the power of the Holy Spirit.

I reject and cancel disappointment and failure in Jesus Christ name.

Father in Jesus Christ name I ask.

I thank you for an answered prayer.

Amen

PRAYER FOR GOD TO LEAD YOUR WAYS

Lord God Almighty, I bring my days, weeks, months and seasons before you and I ask in the name of Jesus, that you order my steps and direct my paths.
Lead me out of temptation and deliver me from evil.
Go ahead of me and level every valley before me.
Uproot every mountain before me and make every crooked path before me straight.
Make me invincible to the forces of darkness.
Let no wicked and unreasonable person attend to me.
God Almighty may your favour be with me.
May your presence go with me.
Deliver me from any pit and trap that has been set for me.
Deliver me from any net that has been spread for my feet.
May those who dug the pit, laid the trap and spread the net be caught by their own snares.
Father, I ask that may my feet not strike against a stone to cause me to fall.
God Almighty may my feet trample upon snakes and scorpions.
Lord God Almighty, put my feet on a broad path and lead me into victory and glory.
Lead me to greener pastures and still waters.

Let everything that I do and am involved in be an absolute blessing unto me.

Give me the wisdom, knowledge and understanding that it will take for me to be successful this season.

Oh Lord God Almighty, deliver me from any delusions, mistakes and foolishness.

Help me Holy Spirit to make wise choices and decisions.

Let me be fruitful and efficient.

Let these my days be an absolute success.

In Jesus Christ name I have prayed. Amen

PRAYER FOR THE CURRENT OR THE NEXT YEAR

Father in heaven in the name of Jesus I bring before you the year …… and I commit it into your hands.
May this year be more glorious to me than all the previous years.
May this year be a more blessed year than all the previous years.
May this year be a more fruitful year than all the previous years.
Oh Lord God, may all that I have suffered in previous years not repeat themselves this year.
Father in heaven, may things that have fought and succeeded against me in the previous years, not succeed against me again.
I declare and decree that affliction shall not happen for the second time against me, in the name of Jesus.
I declare that I am more than a conqueror and that I am victorious.
This year may I grow in wisdom, understanding, knowledge and stature.
I commit all my choices and the decisions that I will make in the year …… into your hands.
Lord, I ask that help me to make wise and fruitful choices and decisions.
May my decisions and choices be a blessing unto me.
Let my choices and decisions come from you.

May my choices and decisions be of you and may they be by you.

Father in heaven, I also ask that order my steps and direct my paths.

Lord, let you hornets go ahead of me and throw my enemies into confusion.

May I never be in the wrong place at the wrong time or in the right place at the wrong time.

Lead me out of temptation and deliver me from evil.

Father, connect me with divine helpers.

Let this year be a better year for me than all my previous years.

Let the evils, disadvantages and failures that I suffered in previous years not repeat themselves this year.

May I know you this year more than I did before.

Father, become much more real and tangible to me than you have ever been.

Let the year …… be a more peaceful year than all the previous years.

Oh Lord God, let the year …… be a glorious year.

Let it be a year of progress and of success.

Let it be my Kairos moment for the answers to my prayer requests.

Let it be the year that I will break through.

Let it be the year that I will persist, in the name of Jesus.

Oh Lord God Almighty, as we enter into next year, let me never be disappointed in any shape or form.

Let me not experience the struggles and the disappointment of the previous year.
In the name of Jesus, I pray
Amen

PRAYER FOR HEALING

Father in the name of Jesus I pray to you.
Father in heaven I thank you for the gift of life.
I thank you for your mercies and loving kindness.
I thank you for your compassion and the gift of healing.
Father, I ask that forgive me of any sins that I have committed which have resulted in this sickness.
I repent of these sins, acquit me from this sin and wash me with the blood of Jesus.
Father, I also ask that you deliver me from all evil effects and consequences of these sins.
And also deliver all people from the evil effects and consequences of these sins.
I thank you for the forgiveness of my sins.
Father, I ask in the name of Jesus that you have mercy on me and heal me of this illness
............(Name) right now.
May your healing virtue enter me now to make me whole.
May I recover from this sickness and may my state not worsen.
Whatever the root cause of these sickness is I command it to wither right now, in the name of Jesus.
Father, deliver me from the root cause of this sickness.

63

Whatever power or spirit is behind this sickness .... (Name) in the name of Jesus, I bind you this power and I command you to leave and go to the abyss now.

Father, deliver me from these powers and spirits.

Whatever activities, systems, altars, high places…etc. are behind this sickness, I command them to be destroyed by fire and earthquake in the name of Jesus.

Father, deliver me from all the evil effects and consequences of these activities.

You this sickness .... (Name) I command you in the name of Jesus to come out of my body, spirit and soul now.

I pull you from your foundation in me and reject you.

In the name of Jesus, I command you my body, spirit and soul to receive the healing of God and to be healed from this .... (Name) right now.

Father in heaven have mercy on me; heal me and make me whole.

Jesus Christ, out of your compassion heal me now.

Holy Spirit let your healing power heal me now.

I receive the healing now in Jesus Christ name.

I declare that there is balm in Gilead and that by the stripes of Jesus I am healed.

In the name of Jesus, I will begin to do now what I could not do because of this sickness.

Thank you, Lord, for the healing in Jesus Christ name. Amen

PRAYER AGAINST DEMONIC ATTACKS

Father in heaven I pray to you in the name of Jesus.
Father, I thank you for your mercies and grace.
I thank you for your love and the plans that you have for me.
Plans to prosper me and give me a future.
I thank you for all that you have done for me.
Despite the challenges and difficulties, if it had not been you on my side, it would have been worse.
Father, I ask that deliver me from these demonic attacks that I'm suffering from .... (Describe)
Whatever has transpired in the realms of the spirit and of the physical by which ....,(Describe)
I ask that may you destroy it and deliver me from having ....(Describe)
Father you are the Lord, my deliverer, deliver me from the cause of these ....(Describe)
Deliver me from these ....(Describe)
Jesus, you came to set the captives free; deliver me from the captivity of the spirits and humans who are behind me having ....(Describe)
Deliver me from the captivity of any altars and systems that are causing me to have......(Describe)
Deliver me from any evil covenants and blood line patterns that have result in me having ....
(Describe)

Deliver me from the captivity of having……… (Describe)

Father, command your angels regarding me.

Take up your shield and buckler and come to my aid.

Deliver me from those who are too strong for me.

Fight against those who are fighting against me.

And contend against those who are contending against me.

Command your angels to wrestle those who are wrestling against me and grant me victory over them.

Save me father from ……………(Describe)

Deliver my poor soul from these evil people and occurrences.

You are my hope.

My trust is in you.

Of course, your hands are not too short to rescue me from these …………(Describe) and heal me from ……………(Describe)

Have compassion on me and save me.

Be merciful unto me and save me.

In the name of Jesus Christ of Nazareth, Satan I bind you regarding me.

I command you to take your hands off me, in the name of Jesus Christ.

Any spells, enchantments, divinations, curses, hypnotisms, manipulations, witchcraft activities, demonic rituals, evil words and evil predictions…etc. that are behind this …………… (Describe)

In the name of Jesus, by the blood of Jesus I cancel them now and I revoke and declare them void.

Whatever evil these activities have set in motion against me and causing ....(Describe)
I halt it now and reverse it back to sender in the name of Jesus, by fire.
Any altars, high places, shrines, grooves, walls of Jericho, strongholds or voodoo shrines
That have been established against me, to bring this attack about, I command them to be destroyed by fire and by a violent earthquake right now, in the name of Jesus Christ.
Whatever has been set in motion and is maintaining this attack against me,
I halt it and reverse it back to sender now in the name of Jesus Christ.
You evil spirit that comes and attacks me, I bind you right now in the name of Jesus Christ.
I invoke and command the consuming fire of the Holy Spirit
And the blood of Jesus to be activated against you now, in the name of Jesus.
You human spirit that comes to attack me and causes me to ....(Describe)
I bind you and I invoke and command the consuming fire of the Holy Spirit and the blood of Jesus to be activated against you, in the name of Jesus.
Angels of the Lord strike them down.
Today I come against you my enemies, whoever and whatever you are, in the name of Jesus and by the power of the Holy Spirit.

May you be destroyed.

May you wither.

As wax melts before fire, may you be destroyed.

I declare that from now on, none of the weapons fashioned against me shall prosper,

In the name of Jesus Christ.

No divination against me shall prosper any more, in the name of Jesus.

For the Lord God Almighty is my shield and protector.

I loose my body, spirit, soul and life from any form of imprisonment that I am in now.

And also from any stronghold that has been established against me, in the name of Jesus Christ.

I command it to scatter and be broken down now by a violent earthquake, in the name of Jesus Christ

I command it to be broken and to scatter now by the angelic ministration of the Lord.

I loose myself and set my body, spirit, soul and life free now.

For the Lord has set me free by His blood.

Now I command the ....(Describe) that happens to me to cease forever now, in Jesus Christ name.

I will not suffer from that again.

Now I command that return now whatever is of mine that you have stolen

Been it my joy, money, marriage, health, blessings …etc. in the name of Jesus, by the power of the Holy Spirit.

Satan you have been caught by the revelation of the word of God.
Take your hands off it now in the name of Jesus.
Angels of the Lord, go and bring it now.
I receive my joy, money, marriage, health, blessings…etc. now in the name of Jesus.
Oh Lord, restore unto me all that my enemies have stolen from me.
Precious Jesus, sweet Holy Spirit, please stand on these my prayers
And intercede on my behalf and intervene in my life.
Father in heaven, may your will be done in these prayers as it is in heaven.
I thank you for an answered prayer.
In Jesus name I have prayed
Amen

PRAYER AGAINST WITCHES / WIZARDS AND WITCHCRAFT ACTIVITIES

Father in heaven I pray to you in the name of Jesus.
Father, I thank you for your mercies and grace.
I thank you for your love and the plans that you have for me.
Plans to prosper me and to give me a future.
I thank you for all that you have done for me.
Despite the challenges and difficulties, if it had not been you on my side, it would have been worse.
I thank you for the power and authority you have given me by your word, over all the powers of Satan.
I also thank you for the name of Jesus that you have given me to cast out and trample over snakes and scorpions, by the power of the Holy Spirit.
Father, I ask that you deliver me from witches and witchcraft covens.
Deliver me from their evil plans and agenda.
Deliver me also from their rituals and activities.
Lord, let the witches and witchcraft covens that have assembled against me wither.
Whoever these witches are, whatever their coven, wherever their meeting place and whatever their tokens and altars are,
I ask that let them be destroyed now and be found no more.

Many are these witches that have gathered against me; arise and destroy them.

Save me from them.

They surround me like dogs, snarling and attacking me.

Looking for a way to destroy me.

They mean evil and ruin for me.

But you, Lord, save and deliver me.

Take out your shield and javelin and come to my aid.

In the name of Jesus, by the power of the Holy Spirit.

You witches that have gathered against me, I command the Holy Ghost consuming fire against you.

Be consumed by fire, fire, fire, fire, fire, fire now.

In the name of Jesus, by the power of the Holy Spirit, I command the Holy Ghost consuming fire against your coven and place of meeting now.

May it be consumed by fire, fire, fire, fire, fire, fire now.

I command the consuming fire against your tokens and your altars now.

May they be consumed by fire, fire, fire, fire, fire, fire now.

Whatever spirit by which you witches operate with, I cripple it in the name of Jesus.

Whatever demons by which they operate with, I bind them now in the name of Jesus.

In the name of Jesus Christ, by the power of the Holy Spirit, with the blood of Jesus Christ.

I nullify any witchcraft rituals, spells, curses, evil words, evil predictions, charms, magic and agendas against me.

In the name of Jesus Christ, by the power of the Holy Spirit, with the blood of Jesus Christ.

I command any witchcraft snares, plots, agendas and activities against me to backfire and return to sender.

Oh Lord God Almighty, whenever they call forth my name, take my picture or present anything of mine to call forth

My spirit, my body or my soul or to send forth any curses or evil against me,

May it not succeed, but rather be answered by the consuming fire.

In the name of Jesus Christ, by the power of the Holy Spirit, with the blood of Jesus Christ.

I invoke and deploy the consuming fire into the realms of the spirit to be activated

Against any witches and witchcraft covens whenever they gather.

To call forth my name, take my picture or to present anything of mine to call forth my spirit, my body or my soul.

Or to send forth any curses or evil against me.

In the name of Jesus Christ, by the power of the Holy Spirit, with the blood of Jesus Christ.

I command any witchcraft activities against me to be destroyed by fire right now.

Been it spells, curses, charms, rituals, manipulations or agents. Be destroyed be fire now.

Whatever these activities have set in motion, I halt it right now and I nullify it by the blood of Jesus.
I command it to reverse back to sender.
Oh Lord, arise and deliver me from them.
Make me invisible to them and their monitoring devices.
Let them be found no more in this life.
As wax melts before fire, let them be destroyed.
In the name of Jesus.
I declare and decree that no witchcraft weapon fashioned against me shall prosper.
For the Lord is my shield and protector.
No divination against Jacob shall prosper.
No divination against me shall prosper.
In the name of Jesus Christ.
Father, I thank you for an answered prayer.
Amen

PRAYER AGAINST ALTARS

Father in heaven I thank you.
I thank you for all that you have done for me
And for all that you are doing.
Father, in the name of Jesus I pray against any altars that are against me.
I ask that you deliver me from them.
Today, let those altars catch fire and be broken into pieces.
Deliver me from anything that these altars are enforcing against me.
Oh Lord, whether these altars are in my mother's lineage or father's lineage,
whether these altars are in my partner's mother's lineage or my partner's father's lineage,
Whether these altars are in my community or country,
Wherever these altars are and come from,
Deliver me from them and their works completely.
In the name of Jesus Christ
By the power of the Holy Spirit,
You altars from my mother or father's lineages,
You altars from my partner's mother's or father's lineage,
You altars from my community and country,
You altars that are anywhere at all,
That are against me and my interests,

Be destroyed now, in Jesus name.
Be broken into piece by a violent earthquake now.
I command the Holy Ghost fire against you now
In the name of Jesus.
May the earth open and swallow you now.
Whoever is behind those altars I command the consuming fire against you.
As wax melts before fire may you be destroyed now.
Whatever, you these altars, are enforcing against me,
In the name of Jesus
I cancel it, I revoke it, I halt it
And I reverse it back to sender.
Oh God Almighty, deliver me from these altars and their agendas against me.
May they have no more influence in my life.
You evil spirit that these altars have invoked against me,
I bind you now in the name of Jesus.
I command you to go to the abyss now.
I invoke the blood of Jesus between you and those condemned altars.
In the name of Jesus,
Your stronghold and power base are demolished, in the name of Jesus.
Therefore, leave and go in the name of Jesus.
I forbid you to ever return, in the name of Jesus.
Whatever you have set in motion against mc,
Today I halt and reverse it back to sender, in the name of Jesus.

Thank you, father, for delivering me from these altars.
In Jesus Christ name,
Amen.

PRAYER TO CAST OUT DEMONS FROM SELF

Father in heaven, in the name of Jesus Christ I pray.
I thank you for your mercies and grace.
I thank you for the blood of Jesus and for the power of the Holy Spirit.
I thank you for the power and authority you have given me by your Word over demons.
I also thank you for the name of Jesus that you have given me to cast out demons, by the power of the Holy Spirit.
Father, I ask that deliver my body, spirit, soul and life from any demons.
Set me free from their captivity.
Cleanse my body, spirit, soul and life of them for I am your temple.
Father, deliver me from whatever has given them the right to be in me, been it sin, evil covenants, curses, occult involvement, sex, my bloodline…etc.
Oh Lord, rid my body, spirit, soul and life
Of any point of contact, root, foundations and doors by which these demons have entered me.
And set me free from them and from their works.
You demons in me, in the name of Jesus Christ and by the power of the Holy Ghost,
I bind you now and I rebuke you.

I command you to come out of me now and go to the abyss by fire, in Jesus Christ name.

Whatever gave you the right to be in me, I revoke it in the name of Jesus and by the blood of Jesus.

Whatever you are standing on to be in me today, I revoke it in the name of Jesus and by the blood of Jesus.

I command it to be destroyed now and to scatter by fire.

Whatever evil you have set in motion against me and in me, I halt it right now in the name of Jesus and I reverse it back to sender.

I command you to come out of me and go to the abyss.

I command you to come out with all that is yours and of you, now, in the name of Jesus, by fire, by fire, by fire.

My body is not yours anymore.

It is now the temple of God.

Christ has bought my body with His blood.

Therefore, in the name of Jesus, by the blood of Jesus, get out, go now and never come back again.

Precious Jesus, please cleanse my body and set it in order.

Restore it to its former glory.

Thank you, Father for delivering me from these demons.

I soak my body, spirit, soul and life in the blood of Jesus.

Father, please cover me and form a hedge around me
In Jesus Christ name I pray
Amen.

PRAYER TO CAST OUT DEMONS FROM A PERSON

Father in heaven, in the name of Jesus Christ I pray.
I thank you for your mercies and grace.
I thank you for the blood of Jesus and for the power of the Holy Spirit.
I thank you for the power and authority you have given me by your Word over demons.
I also thank you for the name of Jesus that you have given me to cast out demons, by the power of the Holy Spirit.
Father, I ask that deliver the body, spirit, soul and life of .... (Name) from any demons.
Set .... (Name) free from their captivity.
Cleanse .... (Name) body, spirit, soul and life of them for they are your temple.
Father, deliver ....(Name) from whatever has given them the right to be in him/her, been it sin, evil covenants, curses, occult involvement, sex, their bloodline...etc.
Oh Lord, rid .... (Name) body, spirit, soul and life of any point of contact, root, foundation and door by which these demons have entered in ....(Name)
And free ....(Name) from them and their works.

You demons in ...., (Name) in the name of Jesus Christ and by the power of the Holy Ghost, I bind you now and I rebuke you.

I command you to come out of .... (Name) now and go to the abyss by fire in Jesus Christ name.

Whatever gave you the right to be in .... (Name) I revoke it in the name of Jesus and by the blood of Jesus.

Whatever you are standing on within ....(Name) today I revoke it in the name of Jesus and by the blood of Jesus.

I command it to be destroyed now and to be scattered by fire.

Whatever evil you have set in motion against .... (Name) and in .... (Name) I halt it right now in the name of Jesus and I reverse it back to sender.

I command you to come out of .... (Name) and go to the abyss.

I command you to come out with all that is yours and of you now in the name of Jesus, by fire, by fire, by fire.

.... (Name) body is not yours anymore.

It is now the temple of God.

Christ has bought ....(Name) body with His blood.

Therefore, in the name of Jesus, by the blood of Jesus, get out now, go and never come back again.

Precious Jesus, please cleanse .... (Name) body and set it in order.

Restore it to its former glory.
Thank you, Father, for the deliverance from these demons.
I soak the body, spirit, soul and life of ………
(Name) in the blood of Jesus.
Father, please cover ………(Name) and form a hedge around ………(Name)
In Jesus Christ name I pray
Amen.

PRAYER TO CAST OUT DEMONS FROM A PLACE

Father in heaven, in the name of Jesus Christ I pray.
I thank you for your mercies and grace.
I thank you for the blood of Jesus and for the power of the Holy Spirit.
I thank you for the power and authority you have given me by your Word over demons.
I also thank you for the name of Jesus that you have given me to cast out demons, by the power of the Holy Spirit.
Father, I ask that deliver this place .... (Name) from any demons.
Set this place .... (Name) free from its captivity.
Cleanse .... (Name) of these demons and make this place your holy ground.
Father, deliver .... (Name) from whatever has given them the right to be here, been it sin, evil covenants, curses, occult involvement, previous owner's activities…etc.
Oh Lord, rid .... (Name) of any point of contact, root, foundations and doors by which these demons have entered .... (Name)
And free this place .... (Name) from these demons and their works.
You demons in this ...., (Name) in the name of Jesus Christ and by the power of the Holy Ghost,

I bind you now and I rebuke you.
I command you to come out of this .... (Name) now and go to the abyss by fire, in Jesus Christ name.
Whatever gave you the right to be in this .... (Name) I revoke it in the name of Jesus and by the blood of Jesus.
Whatever you are standing on within this .... (Name) today I revoke it in the name of Jesus and by the blood of Jesus.
I command it to be destroyed now and to be scattered by fire.
Whatever evil you have set in motion against .... (Name) and in this .... (Name) I halt it right now in the name of Jesus and I reverse it back to sender.
I command you to come out of this .... (Name) and go to the abyss.
I command you to come out with all that is yours and of you now in the name of Jesus, by fire, by fire, by fire.
This .... (Name) is not yours anymore.
It is now of God.
By the blood of Jesus, I exercise control over it.
Therefore, in the name of Jesus, by the blood of Jesus, get out now, go and never come back again.
Precious Jesus, please cleanse this .... (Name) and set it in order.
Restore it to its former glory and let it be a place of peace and blessing.

Thank you, Father, for the deliverance from these demons.
I soak this ……… (Name) in the blood of Jesus.
Father, please cover it and form a hedge around it.
In Jesus Christ name I pray
Amen.

PRAYER TO SANCTIFY AND BLESS A PLACE/THING

Father in heaven, in the name of Jesus I pray to you.
I thank you for this ....(Name)
This is not a small thing but a blessing.
I give you glory, and I praise you for this.
Father, I ask that bless this ....(Name)
Sanctify it and let it be a blessing unto me.
In the name of Jesus, I command the Holy Ghost consuming fire onto this ....(Name)
Let it consume any demonic attachment and point of contact connected to this item and is on it.
Any spirit associated and connected to this
.... (Name) I bind you right now and I command you to leave, in the name of Jesus.
In the name of Jesus, I sprinkle and plead the blood of Jesus on this .... (Name) to break any curses, spells, evil covenants, charms and any other evil associated with it.
I declare that this .... (Name) will only be a blessing unto me and for me, in the name of Jesus.
Father, let your presence and glory rest on this
............(Name)
I thank you for an answered prayer, in Jesus Christ name.
Amen

PRAYER FOR GOD'S INTERVENTION IN A SITUATION

Father in heaven, I pray in the name of Jesus.
Father in heaven, I thank you for your mercies and grace.
Despite the difficulties and the challenges, if it had not been you on my side, it would have been worse.
Father, I bring before you this situation of/about .... (Case) and I ask for your divine intervention in my favour.
Lord God Almighty, if you don't intervene in this situation, then it will be over for me.
My hope, my faith and my trust are in you.
Because there is nothing too hard for you to do and also your hands are not too short to save.
Oh God, with you all things are possible.
Therefore, intervene on my behalf in this ....(Case)
Turn things around .... (Case) in my favour.
Influence the people, the systems, the decision process and all that is connected to this .... (Case) in my favour.
Let every lie and conspiracy against me in this .... (Case) come to light.
Let anything that they are holding against me be considered foolishness and nullify it.

Let my fears about this .... (Case) never come to pass.

Mighty God, step into it and intervene.

Any evil spirits that are behind this situation, I bind and rebuke you in the name of Jesus.

I command you to loose your power and influence in this ....(Case) in the name of Jesus.

Whatever evil that you have set in motion against me in this...............(Case)

I halt and reverse it back to sender, in the name of Jesus.

Lord God Almighty, deliver me from all evil spirits and attacks regarding this ....(Case)

Whatever I did or did not do by which this ....(Case) has arisen, I repent of it.

Please acquit me of it and deliver me from its consequences.

I declare that in the name of Jesus, by the power of the Holy Spirit and by the mercies and grace of God, that this ....(Case) will not destroy me.

It shall not be my end and my fears shall not come to pass.

Thus, whatever is meant for evil, God turn it for my good.

Father in heaven, I thank you for an answered prayer.

In Jesus Christ name I pray.

Amen

PRAYER FOR THE HOLY SPIRIT

Father in heaven I thank you.
I thank you for sending your Holy Spirit into the world.
Father, today I ask in the name of Jesus Christ that give me the gift of the Holy Spirit that you promised to us.
Baptise me in the Holy Spirit with the evidence of speaking in tongues.
Only you can give me the Holy Spirit.
Send your Spirit to come and live in me.
Holy Spirit come and live in me.
Come upon me.
Fill me up.
Father let me be filled with your Spirit.
As you did for them in Acts 2:4, Acts 8:17 and John 20:22,
please do same for me as well.
I thank you for an answered prayer.
In Jesus Christ name I have prayed.
Amen

PRAYER TO BE FILLED WITH THE HOLY SPIRIT

Father in heaven, I thank you.
I thank you for your Holy Spirit.
Precious Jesus, I thank you for going in order that the Holy Spirit be sent.
Sweet Holy Spirit, I thank you for coming.
Father, I ask in the name of Jesus Christ, fill me with your Holy Spirit.
Holy Spirit fill me up.
Father let me be full of the Holy Spirit.
Empty me of anything that is not of you and anything that am full of.
Fill me with your Spirit, Father, and empty me of self.
May you unblock my spiritual well and fill me with your Holy Spirit.
Holy Spirit fill me up,
Let me be drunk of you.
Overshadow me.
As the days and weeks goes by, let me be more and more full of you and nothing else.
I thank you for an answered prayer.
In Jesus Christ name I pray.
Amen.

PRAYER FOR SALVATION

Thank you, my Father in heaven.
Thank you God Almighty for sending your son Jesus Christ to die for me.
Thank you, Jesus, for coming to die for me.
I .... (name) accept that I am a sinner.
And that I need Jesus Christ.
I repent of all my sins.
I ask that you forgive me of my sins.
Wash me with the blood of Jesus and acquit me of my sins.
I .... (name) denounce the world and Satan.
I .... (name) accept Jesus Christ as my Lord and Saviour.
And I confess that Jesus is the Son of God.
Please write my name in the Book of Life.
And may it forever be in it.
Send your Holy Spirit to come and dwell in my heart.
Holy Spirit, I .... (name) open the door of my heart to you.
Come and live in me.
And fill me up.
I .... (name) declare that I am for Christ now.
Thank you for my salvation.
In Jesus Christ name I have prayed.
Thank you for an answered prayer. Amen

PRAYER FOR WISDOM, KNOWLEDGE & UNDERSTANDING

Father in heaven I thank you.
Father in the name of Jesus Christ I pray.
Lord God Almighty, I ask for wisdom, knowledge and understanding.
Your Word says by wisdom a house is built.
And by understanding it is established.
And by knowledge the rooms are filled.
For the house of my life to be built, established and filled, I need wisdom, knowledge and understanding.
Therefore, give unto me the wisdom, knowledge and understanding that I lack.
Give unto me the wisdom, knowledge and understanding that I will need in this life.
Give unto me my own kind of wisdom, knowledge and understanding, that I will need for my life.
Holy Spirit, help me to seek wisdom, knowledge and understanding.
Show me what is wisdom, knowledge and understanding.
Help me to receive and embrace wisdom, knowledge and understanding.
May I not reject wisdom, knowledge and understanding.
The more I age, the more, wiser, knowledgeable and understanding may I be.

Deliver me from any foolishness and replace it with wisdom.
Let wisdom be the principal thing in my life.
May I be as wise as the serpent.
Deliver me from any ignorance.
May I not perish because of lack of knowledge.
Make me a person of knowledge and deliver me from misunderstandings.
Give unto me an understanding heart.
Give me the wisdom that comes from above.
Let me not accept the wisdom of this world, which contradicts the wisdom that comes from above.
Any wisdom that I have but is not truly wisdom but foolishness, today I reject it and I accept your wisdom.
Any knowledge that I have built, which is false and wrong, today I reject it and I accept your knowledge.
Any understanding that I have that is twisted, today I reject it and I accept your understanding.
Oh God, let the Spirit of wisdom, knowledge and understanding rest upon me.
In Jesus Christ name I ask.
I thank you for an answered prayer.
I receive it now
 Amen.

PRAYER ABOUT ONE'S MINDSET

Father in heaven I thank you.
I thank you for your mercies and grace.
I bring before you my mindset and I commit it into your hands.
Your Word says as a man thinks so is he.
Father in the name of Jesus Christ, I ask that you help me to think very well and in an excellent manner.
Father, touch my mind right now and give me the mind of Christ.
Cause my mind to think well.
Cause my brain to function well.
Deliver my brain from any illness and alteration.
May you set my brain to its original setting.
In the name of Jesus Christ, by the power of the Holy Spirit, I take captive every mindset, thinking pattern, imagination, knowledge and speculation that I have, which is not of God and I make it obedient to Christ.
I super impose the knowledge of Christ unto it.
Father, deliver and heal me from anything that is affecting my mind and brain negatively.
Being it mindsets, thinking patterns, imaginations, knowledge, speculations, misunderstandings, education, indoctrination, cultural beliefs, lifestyle…

Any substance abuse or chemicals that I have ingested…
Any demonic manipulations, attacks or spells…
Mind control programming, propaganda, advertisements…
Father, give me a sound mind.
Give me a perfect mind.
Give me a Godly mind.
Give me a clean mind.
Give me the mind of Christ.
Help me to think well Holy Spirit.
Show me and lead me to a better way of thinking.
And better thinking patterns.
I declare that I have a sound and perfect mind and the mind of Christ.
That my brain functions perfectly, in the name of Jesus Christ.
I thank you for an answered prayer.
In Jesus Christ name I pray,
Amen.

PRAYERS FOR BEING SUCCESSFUL AND PROSPEROUS

Father in heaven I thank you.
I thank you for how far you have brought me.
I thank you for your mercies and grace.
Lord God Almighty, I ask that make my life a successful and prosperous one.
Lead me and deliver me from failure.
Grant me success in my day-to-day dealings and activities.
Lead me on paths and into activities.
That will bring me success and prosperity.
Let me not be a failed person in this community and in this world.
Let me not fail as a .... (mention your gender) in this world.
Let me not fail in this .... (mention any venture you are involved in – as many as possible, such as business, exams, applications, …etc.)
In the name of Jesus and by the power of the Holy Ghost,
I command any anti-success and anti-prosperous Systems, schemes, activities, altars, covenants and demonic activities against me to be destroyed by fire.
In the name of Jesus and by the power of the Holy Ghost,

I command any anti success and anti-prosperous strongholds, limitations, embargoes and walls of Jericho against me, to be destroyed now by fire and a violent earthquake.
Any demon that is against me being successful and prosperous,
I bind you now in the name of Jesus and by the power of the Holy Spirit.
Loose your hold and go to the abyss.
Whatever evil that has been set in motion against me not to be successful and prosperous,
I halt it in Jesus Christ name and I reverse it back to sender.
Oh Lord, deliver me from anything that is preventing me from being successful and prosperous.
Fight against those who are fighting against my success and prosperity.
Let everything that I do become successful and prosperous.
I declare that I am a success and I am prosperous.
All that I do shall prosper.
In the name of Jesus Christ.
Father let me make progress in this life and all that I do.
May I never be stagnant.
May the wind of the Spirit blow in my favour.
Thank you, Father, for an answered prayer.
In Jesus Christ name I pray.
Amen.

PRAYER FOR GOD'S BLESSING

Father in heaven, I thank and praise your name
I thank you for all that you have done
And for all that you are doing
Father, this day in the name of Jesus Christ I ask for your blessings
I ask that may your blessings rest upon me
May I be blessed in my going out and in my coming in
May all that I'm doing and connected to be blessed
Bless the works of my hands
Bless those who bless me
Let my seeds be blessed
May I be a blessing to humanity
Bless me with the blessings of Abraham
May the blessings that makes rich and adds no sorrow be upon me
May I walk in those blessings
Oh Lord, bless me with gold and with silver
Bless me with grain and with oil
Bless me with honey and with balm
Bless me with peace and joy
Let my water and food be blessed
Let my household be blessed
Let my days on this earth be full of blessing
Through me, may many be blessed
By virtue of your blessings,

Let every curse and works of curses cease from my life
In the name of Jesus, by the power of the Holy Spirit
I declare that I am blessed by the Lord
And because of the blessing of the Lord, I cannot be cursed
In Jesus Christ name I have prayed
I thank you for an answered prayer
Amen

PRAYER TO OBEY THE WORD OF GOD

Father in heaven I thank you for your word
I thank you for the teachings of your word
Father, today I ask in the name of Jesus that help me to obey your word
Deliver me from any weakness or pride that causes me not to obey your word
Deliver me from any misunderstanding and mindset that cause me not to obey your word
Deliver me also from any delusions and lies that cause me not to obey your word
Give unto me grace to obey your word
Strengthen me with power and boldness to obey your word
Help me to obey your word immediately
Right now, Lord, any word of yours that I'm not obeying
I ask that make it known to me and help me obey it.
Help and cause me to obey the word of God diligently Holy Spirit
As I obey your word, may I never be at a disadvantage
May it rather be my advantage
May I become successful and prosperous as I obey your word

May your word that I obey always be found to be true in all circumstances

Father, release special love into my heart for your word

Help me to sacrifice and count lost anything that I have to sacrifice in order to be obedient to your word.

Father, deliver me from the systems of this world that makes it difficult for people to obey your word

Deliver me from any temptation and evils that make it impossible for people to obey your word

I ………….. (Name), I am willing to obey the word of God above any other word

I choose to obey the word of God over any other thing

Holy Spirit, help this my will and choice to be fulfilled

Make it possible

In Jesus Christ name I have prayed

Amen

PRAYER FOR THE MANIFESTATION OF GOD'S WORD

Father in heaven I thank you for your word, the Bible, that you have given us.
I also thank you for your prophetic word unto me.
I bring both your logos and rhema word before you
And I ask that your word which is Truth should always be true.
In all situations and against all odds, may your word be found to be true in my life.
May your word that I obey and trust in always be true in my life.
May it not be that your word is false.
The more I obey your word, the more may I prosper.
May it not be that I am at a disadvantage because I obey your word.
Father in heaven, let the schemes and systems that have been put in place
To make it seems as if your word is false, fail.
Father in heaven, let the schemes and systems that have been put in place
To make it seems as if obeying your word would put me at a disadvantage, fail.
May it never succeed regarding me.
Father, as I have chosen to obey your word
And as I obey your word,

May you back your word that I obey with
Success, prosperity and fruitfulness.
Back it with peace, joy and gladness.
Back it with miracles, testimonies, signs and wonders.
Holy Spirit, please lead me into the truth of the word of God.
Father let me understand your word more and give unto me deeper revelation of your word.
Let me see wonderful things in your word.
Strengthen me and help me to obey your word in truth and understanding.
Strengthen and help me to obey all your word with gladness.
As the days go by let me love your word and obey it whole-heartedly.
Lead me out of temptation and deliver me from any circumstances that will cause me to disobey your word.
Father, as I obey your word
Let the promise and blessings of your word be true in my life.
Let me walk in it and experience it.
Let not even one word of yours about me fail.
Let every single one come to pass.
Any adversary of and kind and type that will arise against the fulfilment of your word,
Lord, destroy them.
Let them wither and may they be overridden by your power.

Father, let the fulfilment of your word in my life not delay.
But may it always be fulfilled.
I declare that as I have believed and obeyed the word of God I will rather prosper.
That I will never be at a disadvantage.
All demons saying no to this my request,
I bind you and I command you to go to the abyss now, in the name of Jesus.
Whatever you have set in motion against the fulfilment of the word of God in my life, I revoke it now
And I reverse it back to sender, in the name of Jesus.
I thank you father in heaven for an answered prayer.
In Jesus Christ name I have prayed,
Amen.

PRAYER ABOUT FINANCES

Father in heaven I thank you.
I thank you for your provisions and supplies.
Father, in the name of Jesus I bring my finances before you
And I ask that may my finances stabilise.
I ask that you open financial doors for me
And increase me financially.
Give unto me a particular wisdom for my own financial situation.
Deliver me from lack and debt.
Deliver me from borrowing.
Deliver me from financial wastage.
Deliver me from anything that consumes and wastes my money.
Father, deliver me from any systems that are meant to keep me poor,
Been it spiritual or physical.
Let me live in financial sufficiency and abundance.
Oh Lord, may I not lack and may I not be poor.
As your word says,
By the works of my hands may I be financially sufficient.
Bless the work of my hands.
May it never be that I work but lack money.
May it never be that I work but I'm poor.

In the name of Jesus, by the power of the Holy
Spirit, by the Authority of the scriptures,
I rebuke the devourer of my finances.
I command any altars and demonic or human
systems that oppress people financially,
to be destroyed regarding me, in the name of Jesus.
Oh Lord, seal any holes in my purse, pocket and palms
By which my money drains.
In the name of Jesus Christ,
I exchange my poverty for the riches of Christ Jesus.
Christ Jesus, let the grace that you have released which is –
You became poor that through your poverty I may be rich, be at work in my life.
Father, let your blessings that makes one rich and adds no sorrow be upon me.
Let me manifest this blessing.
Give unto me riches.
For riches come from you.
I declare, in the name of Jesus Christ that I will not be poor.
For the scriptures says,
There should be no poor among you.
I will not be poor in Jesus Christ name.
I shall live in abundance and give to others.
I thank you father in heaven for an answered prayer.
In Jesus Christ name I have prayed,
Amen.

PRAYER FOR IMMIGRATIONAL DOOR

Father in heaven,
I thank you for your mercy and grace.
I thank you for this country .... (name of country)
Father in the name of Jesus, I ask that bless .... (name of country)
Let .... (name of country) forever be a great country.
Father, I would like to be a resident and citizen of this country.
I ask that lead me and direct my path to the road that will make me a resident and citizen of this country.
Show me the best route for me to be a resident and citizen of this country, in my particular circumstances.
Connect me to people who will help me to be resident and citizen of this country.
Let immigration doors open to me in this country.
I also ask that you help me to prepare and to be ready for the opportunity to become a citizen of this country.
Any spirits, powers and systems saying no to this, let them be destroyed now, in the name of Jesus.

Any covenants, curses and altars saying no, let them be destroyed now, in the name of Jesus.
Oh Lord, the earth is yours.
Help me to be established in this land.
Let me never be uprooted from this land,
But may I be fruitful here.
May I be a blessing to this land
And may this land be a blessing to me.
In Jesus Christ name I have prayed.
I thank you for the open doors,
Amen.

PRAYER ABOUT AN IMMIGRATION APPLICATION

Father in heaven,
I thank you for your mercy and grace.
I thank you for this country .... (country)
Father in the name of Jesus, I ask that bless .... (country)
Let .... (country) forever be a great country.
Father, I bring my application to be a resident and citizen of .... (country) before you.
I ask that in the name of Jesus, let the outcome of my application be only one.
Father, let the outcome of my application be a success.
Father in heaven, I invoke the blood of Jesus on my application.
May the voice of the blood speak in favour of my application.
May the blood cancel and make foolish anything on my application by which it will be refused.
May the blood cancel any decision that will be made against me.
Father, may my application find favour before anyone who will look at and work on it.
Father, let the process that my application will go through be in my favour.

In the name of Jesus, by the power of the Holy Spirit, I bind and cancel
Any objection to the success of my application.
I command the doors of .... (country) to be opened unto me,
In the name of Jesus.
Father, open the doors of .... (country) before me.
Father, appoint an angel to go and oversee my application, throughout its process.
In the name of Jesus, I reject any refusal.
I declare that the outcome of my application shall be only one
And that one outcome will be that it is successful
And that I have been granted residency and citizenship of .... (country),
In the name of Jesus.
Father, I thank you for an answered prayer.
In Jesus Christ name I have prayed,
Amen

PRAYER WHEN MINISTERING AT A CHURCH SERVICE

Let the Lord arise and may his enemies be scattered and they that hate Him be destroyed.
Oh Lord God Almighty I bring today's service before you and I commit it into your hands.
I pray and ask that may you establish this service.
May You make this service a successful and fruitful one again.
Today, Lord God Almighty may all who come to this service leave rejoicing, giving you glory and praise.
Father in heaven we do not meet in today's service in our names or of our own accord.
Father in heaven we do not meet as a club or as a secular society or as a group of people to feel good.
But we meet in the name of Jesus Christ and by the power of the Holy Ghost;
We meet as your holy convocation, your sacred assembly.
Therefore, Lord God, may our meeting indeed be with you Lord God Almighty.
May it be in the name of Jesus
And as your Word says that where two or three are gathered in your name, there you are with them,
So may you Christ Jesus be with us in today's service.

May your presence be with us in today's service.
May our meeting today be your mount Zion.
May the place of meeting be your holy grounds.
Father, command your angels regarding today's service.
Father in heaven, I ask in the name of Jesus that you bring every member to today's service.
Bring also the 'should be' members and the 'would be' members.
Lord, bring all who came to last week's services, to today's service.
Also bring all who did not come to last week's services, to today's service.
Father, in today's service and by today's service add to the church men like flocks
And increase the church with they that are being saved.
Lord God Almighty, bring the souls and blow them from the north, south, east and west to this service.
All who have made up their minds that they will not attend today's service for whatever reason, been it excuses, phone calls, complications, entanglements, schemes of the enemy or systems of the world, we cancel and revoke these reasons, in Jesus name.
We command the reasons to be destroyed now.
We set them on fire by the fire of God and we declare those reasons void.
Lord, give them a change of mind and bring them to this service.

Let us record the highest number of attendees to date, in today's service.

Satan in the name of Jesus, I bind you regarding the attendance of today's service and I command you to take your hands off the attendance now.

Angels of the Lord, go and bring them into today's service.

I receive and welcome them into today's service.

God put it in their hearts and minds to come to today's service.

Lord God Almighty as you bring them into today's service

Let none of them come empty handed but may they bring to you your tithes, offerings and donations.

May they give to you generously and truthfully.

Satan, I bind you regarding the tithes, the offerings and the donations that are due to the Lord and the church in today's service.

I command you to take your hands off those now in the name of Jesus.

Angels of the Lord go and bring the tithes, offerings and donations due to the Lord and the church.

I receive it and take it for the Lord and for the church in today's service, in the name of Jesus Christ.

Father, I ask that in today's service, meet each one of them at the point of their needs.

Let no one come and go back the same.

Let no one come and remain the same.

Whatever are their needs, their desires and their hopes,
Whatever faith, trust, and belief they have for coming,
May you uphold them and may their faith, trust and belief not be dashed into pieces, but may you meet them at the point of their need.
Father, I ask that as they come, work on each one of them.
Work in each one of them and work regarding each one of them.
Father as they come, I pray that meet each one of them.
May they leave rejoicing and giving you praise and glory.
Lord God as they come to today's service, speak to them, hear their prayers, and minister to them.
May you become real and tangible to them.
Lord God Almighty do good unto all who come to today's service.
Show them mercy and be gracious to them.
May your mercies be in today's service.
May your grace be in today's service.
Lord, favor all who come to today's service and show them your loving kindness.
May your love and kindness be in this service.
Father in heaven may your presence be in today's service.
May your Holy Spirit be in today's service.

May you be there and may you be at work in today's service.

Precious Jesus, may you be in our midst in today's service.

Father, may your angels be in the service.

Command them regarding the service.

Command the heavens. the earth, the waters and beneath the earth regarding today's service.

Father, let everything in this town and country all work for the benefit and in favor of today's service.

Let everything in the physical and spiritual world work for the benefit and favor of today's service.

Father in today's service, let your wind of refreshment that causes people's dry bones to come back to life,

Blow in the service and let it blow on all who come.

And let it blow in their lives and cause any good thing that is dead in their lives to come alive, in the name of Jesus.

Father let your living waters flow in this service.

Let the rivers that flow from your altar;

The rivers that bring fruitfulness, flow in today's service and into the lives of all who are coming and may they begin to be fruitful.

Oh Lord, let the heavens open over this service and let it rain on us.

Let your blessing rain on us

Let your spirit Oh Lord rain on us.

Let your light also shine on us and shine in the service and shine on the lives of all in the service.

Let the light disperse any form of darkness and works of darkness from the service

And from the lives of all who are coming.

Lord God Almighty, may your will be done in the service as it is in heaven and may your kingdom come in the service.

May today's service be in your perfect and absolute will.

May your will be done as it is in heaven, in the lives of all who are coming and may your kingdom come in their lives as it in heaven.

May they be operating in your kingdom dimension.

Father I also bring before you each and every activity that will be done in today's service

Including the prayers, your Word that will be preached, the offerings and the tithes, the communion, the worship and praise songs and the ministration.

I commit all into your hands.

May these activities be pleasing and acceptable unto you.

Let none of these activities be done as rituals or for fun or in vain.

But may the service be a blessing on to us.

May it be for our profit and our benefit.

Oh Lord God Almighty may these activities never be a waste of time or a waste of resources.

Lord, I also bring before you all vessels that will minister in today's service,

Including those leading worship, those leading prayer, those preaching, those reading the Bible and those playing instruments. I also bring before you the camera crew, sound people and social media team and all who will serve in today's service
I ask that you sanctify and purify them.
Empty them of self and fill them with your Spirit.
Let them be full of the Spirit.
Use them mightily in today's service.
Let none of them minister in the flesh.
Let them minister under the anointing and in the name of Jesus, by the power of the Holy Ghost.
Oh Lord God Almighty, I ask that let their service today be a blessing to the church
And may it be pleasing and acceptable to you.
May it be a blessing unto them, in the name of Jesus.
Lord God Almighty, as your people come to the service, speak to them and minister to them.
Let there be miracles, signs and wonders;
May there be deliverance, healing, impartation
And may there be manifestations of your presence and a demonstration of your power in the service.
Let there be prophecy; let your prophetic word be at work.
Let there be words of knowledge and words of wisdom in today's service.
Let there be love in the service.
Oh Lord God Almighty, let your Spirit be at work in today's service.

I pray thee and I asked that as they come to today's service, heal those who need healing.
Those who need deliverance, deliver them.
Those who need miracles, grant them miracles.
Those who need signs and wonders, give them signs and wonders.
Those who need to see your glory or power in any shape or form, let them see it.
Those who need your prophetic word, give them your prophetic word.
Those who need a word of knowledge or word of wisdom, give them a word of knowledge or word of wisdom.
Let them be fed with your knowledge, wisdom and understanding.
Lord, I pray that you purify and cleanse them, work on their minds and hearts.
Let the power by which people are transformed into your image be at work in today's service.
As they come may their lives be transformed for good by this power in the name of Jesus.
Father in heaven, touch their hearts and their minds and their eyes.
Father, back today's service with miracles.
Back it with signs and wonders.
Back it with healing.
Back it with deliverance.
Back it with testimonies.
Back it with manifestations of your presence and demonstrations of your power.

Back it with Church growth.
Back it with salvation.
Back it with words of knowledge and words of wisdom.
Back it with prophecy.
Back it with deliverance.
Let no one come and go back the same, nor remain the same as they came in.
Meet each one of them at the point of their needs.
Let the Lord arise and may his enemies be scattered and they that hate him be destroyed.
Oh Lord God, arise and let your enemies be scattered and they that hate you be destroyed.
Oh Lord God, let the enemies of today's service and they that hate today's service
And they that hate what we are for and what we stand against,
Be destroyed and let them be scattered.
Let them be broken up.
As wax melts before fire let them be destroyed.
Oh Lord, your Word says,
We wrestle not against flesh and blood, but against powers, against principalities, against the rulers of the darkness of this world and against spiritual wickedness…'
Therefore, I ask that wrestle against those powers, principalities, rulers of the darkness of this world and the spiritual wickedness in high places on our behalf.

Fight against them, command your angels against them and grant us victory over them.

Let us possess that which they are wrestling us for, in the name of Jesus, by the power of the Holy Ghost.

Lord your Word also says that 'you will contend against those who contend against us and fight against those who fight against us'.

I pray that you arise Lord and contend and fight against those who are contending and fighting against this service and the interests of the service and against what we will be praying for and also praying against.

Take up your shield and buckler and come to our aid.

Let them be trodden down. Let them be broken right down in the name of Jesus.

Father, let this service be an absolute blessing.

Any demons that have been assigned against us in today's service, or that will rise against this service or the interests of today's service

Or against anyone who is coming to today's service

Or what we will be praying for and against,

In the name of Jesus, by the power of the Holy Ghost, I bind you; I command you to loose your grip and go to the abyss by fire, never to return again.

Whatever you have set in motion against this service, I halt it and reverse it back to sender in the name of Jesus.

Father may it be reversed right now in the name of Jesus.

Any human spirit that is a vessel of these demons and have been assigned against the interests of today's service

Or against those who are coming,

Father, strike these vessels now and destroy them in the name of Jesus.

Any strong man that will lift themselves up or has lifted themselves up against this service in any shape or form,

we bind you in the name of Jesus, by the power of the Holy Ghost.

Be bound now and be broken.

I command you to go to the abyss and never come back again, in the name of Jesus.

Any altars, high places, shrines, grooves, poles, walls of Jericho

Any gates of bronze; any strongholds, limitations or embargos; Any demonic programming or systems that have been lifted up against this service

Or against the interests of this service, I command it to be destroyed right now.

Oh Lord, let there be a violent earthquake and may the grounds open up and swallow them.

May they be destroyed and whatever they are enforcing and maintaining

Be halted, reversed and returned back to sender now,

In the name of Jesus.

Oh Lord, let any enchantments, any divinations, curses, hexes, evil covenants,
Any witchcraft and satanic activities, any magic, charms, hypnotisms, evil prayers, words, directions
Or desires that have been invoked and spoken against this service or the interest of the service in any shape or form, be revoked right now.
In the name of Jesus by the power of the Holy Ghost,
we terminate and cancel these now.
By the blood of Jesus, we nullify them.
Whatever these activities have set in motion against this service We halt, reverse and return back to sender now in the name of Jesus, by the power of the Holy Ghost.
Lord God Almighty, I command the Holy Ghost consuming fire now unto the place of meeting and the entire building.
Let your fire sweep through and may it consume any demonic presence, accursed thing and anything that is not of you now.
Let the service be set ablaze by your fire.
I also invoke the consuming fire into the realms of the Spirit to be activated against
Any schemes or activities and any human or spirit beings that will rise against the service, in the name of Jesus.
In the name of Jesus, I sprinkle the blood of Jesus onto the place of meeting and on the entire building.
By the blood of Jesus, I break any

curses, charms, divinations, embargos, limitations, written words and ordinances or any filthy thing that has been placed or written on the place of meeting.

I wash and clean the entire building with the blood of Jesus.

I invoke the full potency of the blood of Jesus into the service,

on the place of meeting and on anything connected to the service.

Lord, I deploy and invoke the blood of Jesus into the realms of the spirit to be activated against

any person or spirit or activities against this service in any way.

Father in heaven, may your will be done in today's service as it is in heaven and may your kingdom come into this service

Oh Lord, I bring all who will be serving in today's service before you

And I ask that may they be united and not divided.

May we be one body, one spirit, one soul, one mind, one heart and one speech.

Oh Lord God, I pray that let them do all things in love and by the anointing.

Father, I bring my body, my spirit, my soul before you today and I ask you to anoint me for this service.

Empty me of all that is not yours and fill me with all that is of you for today's service.

Let me be your flaming fire.

Lord God Almighty today too, as I go to serve your people,
may it not be me as a mere human being but may it be as your servant and your vessel.
Fill me with your Holy Spirit.
Holy Spirit fill me up, overshadow me.
Jesus, overshadow me and may I be in you and you in me.
Let your mighty hand come upon me and use me in today's service.
Use me to lead and minister to your people.
Use me to manifest yourself and demonstrate your power.
Use me to lead these people before you today in your name.
Let it be you and not be me.
Father, I bring all the scriptures that will be used in today's service before you.
Lord, I ask that you sanctify these scriptures, turning them from your logos word into rhema words.
Lord God Almighty, I also ask that you help me to divide?? your word accurately and may your word that is Truth be found to be the Truth.
Lord, I also ask that you give all who come to the service divine understanding and revelation about the scriptures and all that will be done in the service.
Lord, I pray that you back the scriptures with salvation, repentance, renewal of people's minds, testimonies, signs, wonders and miracles,

as well as healing, deliverance and manifestations of your presence and demonstrations of your power.
Oh Lord, in today's service may you hear and answer our prayers in our favor.
May our attendance of today's service be to our advantage, in the name of Jesus.
Father in today's service impart to your people wisdom, knowledge, understanding, grace, anointing and power, in the name of Jesus Christ of Nazareth.
May I find favor before all who I stand before in today's service.
Lord your word says people judge by what they see. I ask that may their judgment be in my favor and may they receive me as your servant.
Father, I ask that may my words be understood by them and may they be in agreement with them.
Father, let your will be done in today's service as it is in heaven and may your kingdom come into this service.
Oh Lord God Almighty, as they come to this service speak to them, minister to them, touch and meet them at the point of their needs.
Oh God Almighty deliver them from their weaknesses,
impart on them and fill them with the Holy Spirit.
God, become more tangible to them than ever.
I declare and decree, in the mighty name of Jesus Christ of Nazareth, by the power of the Holy Ghost that no weapon fashioned against today's service shall prosper.

I refute every weapon of the enemy against this service.
I declare and decree, in the name of Jesus by the power of the Holy Ghost,
that today's service shall be fruitful and successful. We will leave today's service rejoicing, giving glory and praise to God, in the name of Jesus.
In Jesus Christ name I have prayed.

PRAYER WHEN WORKING IN A CHURCH SERVICE

Father in heaven, I thank you for today's service.
I thank you for the privilege to serve as ……, in today's service.
I ask that let my service be pleasing and acceptable unto you.
Let my service be a blessing to all who come to today's service and also to the church.
Let my service be a blessing unto me and to my household.
I ask that sanctify me and anoint me for today's service.
Purge me and empty me of anything that is not of you.
Fill me with your Spirit and all that is of you.
Anoint me for today's service.
Cause me to serve under your anointing today.
May I be under the influence of the Holy Spirit.
May I serve you today with all my heart and strength.
Help me God, to serve skilfully in today's service.
Deliver me and my service from anything carnal.
As I serve by …….. (Role) use it to minister to your people.
Use it to transmit your power, presence and grace.
Use it to back the service and the ministration of all who will serve and minister in today's service.

By my service, may today's service serve its purpose, according to your will.

May I be of one spirit, one body and one mind with all who are serving in today's service.

May we be unified and not divided.

Father, I also ask that may this service be highly patronized.

I also ask that may this service be fruitful and successful.

Father, I ask that may your will be done in this service and may your kingdom come in this service.

Let this service be pleasing and acceptable unto you.

May today's service be a meeting with you God; the Father, the Son and the Holy Spirit.

Lord God almighty, do not allow anyone's sins to hinder today's service in any shape or form.

Do not allow Satan and evil people to hinder this service in any shape or form.

Do not allow any works of Satan and his agents to hinder today's service.

Let all weapons of the enemy against today's service fail.

Father as I go to the service, I ask that meet me at the point of my need.

Use your servant, use all who will minister, use all activities and your various ways in today's service to meet me at the point of my need.

Work on me, work in me and work regarding me.

Speak to me, teach me your ways and minister to me.

Reach out to me and touch me.

Become more tangible and more real to me than ever.

Command your angels regarding me in today's service.

Let your Holy Spirit locate me in today's service.

Oh Lord, whatever you do in today's service do not leave me out.

Anoint the pastor who will minister in today's service and use him/her mightily to teach your Word and prophecy.

Use him/her to perform miracles and signs and wonders.

Use him/her to heal the sick and cast out devils.

Use him/her to lead many unto salvation.

Use him/her to give words of knowledge and words of wisdom.

Open his/her eyes and put your words in his/her mouth.

I ask that do the same with all people that will serve in today's service in whatever capacity.

By today's service, among other things may you become more real and tangible to me than ever.

May you speak to me.

May you heal and deliver me from all evil.

May you bless me.

May I become holy and righteous.

May I be filled with the Holy Spirit.

May I be imparted with knowledge, wisdom and understanding.

May you hear my prayers and cause the answered prayers to manifest.
May you be merciful and gracious to me.
Do good to me and show me your loving kindness.
Forgive me of my sins and trespasses.
May I not come back the same as how I went in.
Let all activities that I engage in at the service be pleasing unto you and may they be a blessing unto me.
May my attendance in today's service be to my advantage and may it be a blessing unto me.
May my attendance be a blessing unto the church and all who are attending the service.
I declare and decree that today's service will be very successful and fruitful
and that no weapon fashioned against today's service shall prosper.
I refute every weapon of the enemy against today's service.
In Jesus Christ name I have prayed.

PRAYER WHEN ATTENDING CHURCH SERVICE

Father in heaven I thank you for this service today.
I attend this service in the name of Jesus.
I ask that may this service be highly patronized.
I also ask that may this service be fruitful and successful.
Father, I ask that may your will be done in this service and may your kingdom come in this service.
Let this service be pleasing and acceptable unto you.
May today's service be a meeting with you God the Father, the Son and the Holy Spirit.
Lord God almighty, do not allow anyone's sins to hinder today's service in any shape or form.
Do not allow Satan and evil people to hinder this service in any shape or form.
Do not allow any works of Satan and his agents to hinder today's service.
Let all weapons of the enemy against today's service fail.
Father as I go to the service, I ask that you meet me at the point of my need.
Through your servant and all who will minister in today's service
 Through all activities and your various ways in today's service.
Meet me at the point of my needs

Work on me, work in me and work regarding me.
Speak to me, teach me your ways and minister to me.
Reach out to me and touch me.
Become more tangible and more real to me than ever.
Command your angels regarding me in today's service.
Let your Holy Spirit locate me in today's service.
Oh Lord, whatever you do in today's service, do not leave me out.
Anoint the pastor who will minister in today's service and use him/her mightily to teach your word and to prophecy.
Use him/her to perform miracles, signs and wonders.
Use him/her to heal the sick and cast out devils.
Use him/her to lead many unto salvation.
Use him/her to give words of knowledge and words of wisdom.
Open his eyes and put your words in his mouth.
I ask that you do the same with all who will serve in today's service in any capacity.
By today's service, among other things, may you become more real and tangible to me than ever.
May you speak to me.
May you heal me and deliver me from all evil.
May you bless me.
May I become holy and righteous.
May I be filled with the Holy Spirit.

May I be imparted with knowledge, wisdom and understanding.

May you hear my prayers and cause my answered prayers to manifest.

May you be merciful and gracious to me.

Do good to me and show me your loving kindness.

Forgive me of my sins and trespasses.

May I not come back the same as I went in.

Let all activities that I engage in at the service be pleasing unto you and may they be a blessing unto me.

May my attendance in today's service be to my advantage and may it be a blessing unto me.

May my attendance be a blessing unto the church and to all who attend the service.

I declare and decree that today's service will be very successful and fruitful and that no weapon fashioned against today's service shall prosper.

I refute every weapon of the enemy against today's service.

In Jesus Christ name I have prayed.

PRAYER FOR CHURCH GROWTH

Father in heaven, I thank you for (name) ....
Church.
I thank you for all that you have used the church for and all the plans that you have for it.
Father, into your hands I commit the growth of (name) .... church.
Your Word says that neither the one who plants nor the one who waters is anything, but only God is the one who makes things grow.
You God who makes things grow, cause .... (name) to grow.
As long as the days goes by and the weeks goes by, let your church forever continue to grow.
Let it grow in membership, in attendance and in workers.
Let the offerings, tithes and donations also grow
Let the power, anointing and grace also grow.
Father let the church also grow in love for one another and for you.
Let us grow in holiness and righteousness.
I ask for the all-round growth for the church.
Add to (name) .... church men like flocks and increase it with they that are being saved.
Bring faithful and wise people into the church.
Recommend your church to people and lead them to it.

Sweet Holy Spirit, may you be the marketing executive
And promoter of (name) ………… church and bring many people in.
When you bring them, let them remain and be planted in the church.
Whatever causes people to come and never return we cancel it in Jesus Christ name.
The enemy's scheme to mix his agents in with them, we block it in the name of Jesus.
Father, prevent and stop the agents of Satan from coming into (name) ………… church.
Precious Jesus, you said you will build your church and the gates of hell shall not prevail against it.
I therefore ask that you build your church ………… (name) and that the gates of hell may not prevail against it.
Let the gates of hell and its representatives and activities fail against (name) ………… church.
May it never succeed.
Father, let the things that have prevented your churches from growing in this town, city, country and world, been it spiritually or physically
Not succeed with (name) ………… church.
I ask that the more the gates of hell rise against (name) ………… church, the more may they fail and the more may your church ………… (name) be built.

I declare and decree in the name of Jesus that
............(name) shall be built and is being built and the gates of hell shall not succeed against it.

I command any darkness that has been cast over (name) .... church to be dispersed now
By the light that shines into darkness and darkness cannot comprehend it,
Now in the name of Jesus.

I command the eyes of the souls to be open to (name) .... church now, in Jesus Christ name.
In the name of Jesus, by the power of the Holy Spirit
I command any altars, high places, poles, strongholds, walls of Jericho, gates of bronze, embargos, limitations and systems
That are against the growth of (name) .... church, to be destroyed and scattered by fire
And by a violent earthquake now.
In the name of Jesus, by the power of the Holy Spirit
I cancel and nullify any curses, divinations, charms, magic, spells, witchcraft activities, satanic activities, hypnotisms, evil covenants, evil prayers, evil directions, evil words and evil desires against
The growth of (name) .... Church, by the blood of Jesus.

Whatever evil that these systems and activities have set in motion, I halt, reverse and return them back to sender, in the name of Jesus.

Father, I ask that you deliver your church
............(name) from all these systems and activities.
In the name of Jesus, you demons that have been assigned against the growth of (name) .... church,
I bind you now and I command you to go to the abyss now by fire, by fire, by fire.
Whatever evil you have set in motion against the growth of (name) .... church,
I halt it and reverse it back to sender, in Jesus Christ name.
Satan, I bind you regarding the growth of (name) .... church
And I command you to take your hands off it now, in Jesus Christ name.
Angels of the Lord, go and bring the growth.
Father in heaven, deliver your church from these demons and their activities.
Father, fight against all who are fighting against the growth of (name) .... church.
Contend against all who are contending against the growth of (name) .... church.
Wrestle against the powers, principalities, spiritual wickedness in high places and the rulers of the darkness of this world
That are wrestling against the growth of (name) .... church.
May they be defeated and may your church ....(name) be built and may it grow.

Oh Lord God Almighty, into your hands I commit the battle regarding the growth of (name) .... church.

The battle is yours, fight on behalf of .... church.

Command your angels regarding the growth of (name) .... church and let it grow.

Show us what we need to do and what we must refrain from doing in order for your church ....(name) to grow.

The grace by which your church's grow, let that grace be on (name) .... church, that it may grow.

Let (name) .... church grow and become very fruitful.

I thank you for answered prayers in Jesus Christ name.

Amen

GENERAL PRAYER FOR A CHURCH

Father in heaven I thank you for your church
............(name)
Father, I pray for your church .... (name)
And I ask in the name of Jesus Christ, that may your church .... (name) be established and built.
May it grow and never cease to grow.
May it be a church pleasing and acceptable unto you.
May your church .... (name) be a glorious church, not having spot or wrinkle or any such thing,
But be holy and without blemish.
Let ....(name) church indeed be the body of Christ Jesus that it is and may the members indeed become individual member parts of His body.
Holy Spirit, may you indeed be the overseer of .... (name) church.
May your power, presence, gifts, fruits and manifestations be at work in the church.
As a church let the members be of one mind, one thought and one language.
Let us not be divided but let us be united as a church.
Deliver your church from unfaithful and wicked members and servants.
Let them not succeed.
Let your church be a house of prayer and let all nations come and seek you there.

Let it be a place where your people will be fed with wisdom, knowledge and understanding.

May your church ....(name) never be a house of thieves or a place for showing off.

Let your church never lack and let there be ample provision in your church forever.

May every member in the church be one who tithes faithfully and gives generously.

Let your power of transformation be at work in that church.

May every prayer that is prayed in the church be heard and answered by you.

Let your Word come forth in your church with power and authority.

Let your church become the pillar and foundation of truth.

Let the heavens open over your church and let your church be under open heavens.

Let your blessings forever be in the church.

Let the attendance, membership and participation in the church and its activities only be a blessing to all who are involved.

Satan, in the name of Jesus I command you to take your hands of .... (name) church now.

I bind you regarding her now by the power of the Holy Spirit.

In the name of Jesus, by the power of the Holy Spirit

I command any altars, high places, poles, strongholds, walls of Jericho, gates of bronze,

embargos, limitations and systems that are against
............(name) church to be destroyed
And be scattered by fire and by a violent earthquake now.
In the name of Jesus, by the power of the Holy Spirit
I cancel and nullify any curses, divinations, charms, magic, spells, witchcraft activities, satanic activities, hypnotisms, evil covenants, evil prayers, evil directions, evil words and evil desires against
.... (name) church by the blood of Jesus.
Whatever evil that these systems and activities have set in motion, I halt and reverse back to sender in the name of Jesus.
Father, I ask that deliver your church
............(name) from these systems and activities.
In the name of Jesus, you demons that have been assigned against .... (name) church,
I bind you now and I command you to go to the abyss now by fire, by fire, by fire.
Whatever evil you have set in motion against
.... (name) church, I halt it and reverse it back to sender, in Jesus Christ name.
Satan, I bind you regarding the growth of
............(name) church
And I command you to take your hands off it now, in Jesus Christ name.
Angels of the Lord go and bring the growth.
Father in heaven, deliver your church from these demons and their activities.

Father fight against all who are fighting against
.... (name) church.
Contend against all who are contending against
.... (name) church.
Wrestle against the powers, principalities, spiritual wickedness in high places and the rulers of the darkness of this world that are wrestling against
.... (name) church.
May they be defeated and let your church .... (name) be built.
Father, I also ask that any agent that will be sent to come and fight against the church is stopped.
Holy Spirit arrest them, angels of the Lord strike and prevent them from coming.
Lord if you allow them to come for whatever reason, may they not succeed.
Father, any agents who are in the church, let them not succeed but may they be disgraced and be routed out.
May every activity in the church service be a torment to them.
May your consuming fire descend against them whenever they set foot in the church.
Oh Lord God Almighty.
Let your church be your mount Zion.
Let it be your holy grounds.
Let there be testimonies, blessings and riches in the church.
Let there be marriages, jobs, children, celebrations, joy, laughter and liberty in the church.

Let there be miracles, signs and wonders, manifestations of your presence and demonstrations of your power in the church.
Let there be impartations, healings and deliverance in the church.
Let your mercy, grace, loving kindness, goodness, favour and glory be in the church.
Oh Lord I ask again, let there be love in the church.
Let there be holiness and righteousness in the church.
Let your church remain and endure forever for generations upon generations.
In Jesus Christ name I pray
Amen

PRAYER FOR EVANGELISM

Father in heaven I thank you.
I thank you for sending your only begotten Son, Christ Jesus to bring salvation into this world.
Father, in the name of Jesus Christ and by the authority of your Word
I go out to .... (location) for soul winning.
I do not go of my own accord.
Father, I ask that as I go give me souls.
Make me a fisher of men
And let me return with the souls of men.
As I go may the grounds of .... (location) be fertile to me.
May I be received and never rejected.
As I go, let souls attend to me and may I not be despised.
Because I am going to .... (location) for soul winning
Bring those who are being saved and those who will receive your salvation, there today.
Let them cross paths with me
And let them receive your message of salvation for them.
Father, in the name of Jesus, as I go
Use me to turn sinners to righteousness.
Use me to turn back the hearts of backsliders to you.

Use me to pursue people into your house, the Church.
Use me to teach your Word.
Use me for healing, miracles, signs and wonders.
Use me to minister to people that you want ministered to.
Use me for your will and your glory.
Oh Lord, may I not return without the souls of men.
Give me souls.
Put your Word in my mouth for them.
As you have ordained me to be as the light of the world
May I be a bright light there today
And may all who seek the light come to me,
And when they come may they find Jesus, The Light of The World.
May all who are thirsty and seek the living waters come to me today,
And when they come to me
May they find the Living Water, Christ Jesus.
In the name of Jesus, by the power of the Holy Ghost,
I command the consuming fire unto ………… (location)
To consume any demonic presence, any accursed thing and anything against the souls and against me and my purpose.
I invoke and plead the blood of Jesus unto ………… (location)

To revoke and reverse any demonic and evil activities against me, and against my purpose and the souls.

In the name of Jesus Christ, by the power of the Holy Ghost,

I revoke any spells, enchantments, divinations and witchcraft and satanic activities

That have been invoked against me, my purpose and the souls.

Whatever evil that these activities have set in motion against me, my purpose and the souls,

I halt it now and reverse it back to sender.

Any altars, high places, strongholds and walls of Jericho

That have been lifted up against me, my purpose and the souls,

I command them to crumble now by fire and a violent earthquake.

In the name of Jesus, by the power of the Holy Spirit,

Whatever evil that they are enforcing against me, my purpose and the souls,

I halt it now and reverse it back to sender.

Any evils spirit that has been assigned against me, my purpose and the souls,

I bind you now in the name of Jesus.

I command you to go to the abyss now.

I revoke and declare your assignment – failed.

Any human vessels that are coming against me, my purpose and the souls,

Whatever spirit by which they operate,
I bind and gripple it in the name of Jesus.
Father, may their purpose against me and against my purpose and the souls
Fail and be defeated, in the name of Jesus.
Oh Lord God Almighty arise
And fight against those who are and will be fighting against me, my purpose and the souls.
Contend against those who are and will be contending against me, my purpose and the souls.
Your Word says,
We wrestle not against flesh and blood.
I ask in the name of Jesus that wrestle against anything that is not flesh and blood,
Fight against anyone who is and will be fighting against me, my purpose and the souls.
As I go, in the name of Jesus
I take captive of any mindsets, thinking patterns, imaginations and lies
against me, my purpose and the souls
and I bring it under subjection to Christ Jesus
and I superimpose the truth on it.
Holy Spirit fill me up.
Father, let me full of the Holy Spirit.
Anoint me for today's evangelism.
Let your presence go with me.
Let your angels go with me.
Use me mightily
Let no weapon fashioned against me prosper.

Let me return with souls, testimonies and thanksgiving.
I declare and decree that no weapon fashioned against me and my purpose at ………… (location) shall prosper, in the name of Jesus.
I declare and decree that I shall be very fruitful and successful today.
Oh Lord, let your will be done in today's evangelism
As it is in heaven
And may your kingdom come in it.
May today's evangelism be in your perfect will and operate in your kingdom dimensions.
I thank you for answered prayer.
In Jesus Christ name I have prayed
Amen

PRAYER FOR A MAN OF GOD/ PASTOR

Father in heaven, I thank you for ………….. (man of God's name)
I thank you for sending him to me
LORD God Almighty, into your hands I commit
………
I commit his/her body, spirit, soul, life and ministry into your hands
I ask in the name of Jesus that protect and preserve him/her
Order his/her steps and direct his/her path.
Lead him/her from temptation and deliver him /her from evil
Let no weapon fashioning against him/her prosper
Let every attack against him/her and the family fail
May it never be that ………… or his/her family are at a disadvantage because he/she serves you
Fight against those who are fighting against him/her
Contend against those who are contending against him/her
Wrestle against the powers, principalities, spiritual wickedness and the rulers of the darkness of this world wrestling against him/her
Strengthen him/her and keep him/her healthy
May your anointing forever increase on ………
Endure him/her with power and authority

May he/she operate mightily in the gifts of the Holy Spirit
Fill him/her with love for your sheep's and your work
Give him/her divine understanding and revelation of your word
Cause and help him/her to preach and teach your word
With boldness, in power and with authority
Help and lead him/her to divide your word accurately
Let people understand your word that he/she preaches
Let him/her find favour before your people and all who he/she comes across
Let him/her be received and accepted and never be rejected
Use him/her to feed your people with wisdom and understanding
Use him/her to equip the saints for the work of the ministry
Use him/her to turn sinners into repentance
Use him/her to win the lost and bring back backsliders
Use him/her to persuade people into you house
Use him/her to heal the sick and cast out devils
Oh Christ Jesus, the works that you did
May he/she also do
Even greater works than you did may he /she do
By him/her may many be blessed

By him/her let your righteousness spread forth
Let him/her not lack
Let him/her not be poor
Let him/her be successful in all that he/she does
Let him/her finish his/her course very well
May your will be done in his/her life
Have mercy on him/her and be gracious unto him/her
Show him/her your loving kindness and favour him/her
Open the eyes of his/her understanding
Reveal to him/her secrets and mysteries
Let things that have destroyed and stopped your pastors from succeeding, not prevail with him/her
Let him/her not fail where your pastors have failed
Bless him/her and his household
Bless those who bless him/her
Bring people to come and help him/her greatly
Holy spirit, help him/her greatly
By him/her let God become tangible to people
By him/her may God who is real be ever more real to people
By him/her let many believe in Christ Jesus
I thank you for an answered prayer
In Jesus Christ name
Amen

YOU ARE BLESSED